LIBERTY TO THE RESCUE

How Governing for Liberty
Can Get Us Out of
The Mess We're In

John Wendell Ames

This book was written and designed in Word 2010 ®

Front cover art is by SPURGA at fiverr.com

The back cover photo is by Alice Ames Jahn

ISBN: 978-0-578-41410-2

A Living Liberty imprint

Available from Amazon.com and other book stores

Contents

Preface   i

1. What is Liberty?   1

2. What Liberty is not   11

3. The Value of Liberty   15

4. Governing for Liberty   31

5. The Constitution   43

6. Full-Service Government with Liberty   63

7. Politics of Liberty   145

8. Contrary Principles   155

9. Religion   177

10. Liberty and Tough Issues   181

Epilogue   219

Acknowledgments   221

Appendix A: Immigration Risks   223

End Notes   231

Index   247

Preface

Recommitment to the principles of liberty can arrest and cure the extreme polarization, despair, and incivility poisoning our republic. While Americans have been fortunate to enjoy more liberty than most of the world, we rarely appreciate what we have, and so risk losing that and more if we don't practice and defend it.

Liberty can be understood as simple restraints we apply to ourselves as we deal with our fellow citizens. The classical definitions of liberty such as freedom of speech, religion, and private property follow when these restraints also apply to government. Liberty is appreciated from personal, cultural, spiritual, and even cosmic perspectives. A dozen principles common in American politics but to some degree contrary to liberty are visited to see their appeal and their risks.

Government policies are observed through the lens of liberty to judge their suitability for a free people. We will learn that a strong government is needed to preserve liberty, but that same government has the potential to destroy it. Our task is learning how to control this beast.

This is neither a partisan polemic nor a history, but an informal discussion of liberty and how it can guide policy. The origins of liberty and government are skimmed over in only enough detail to set the stage. The focus is primarily on how liberty can work in the here and now with real people facing real life. Current issues are explored to discover improved policies.

John Wendell Ames   Ashland, Oregon, August 2018

John Wendell Ames							Liberty to the Rescue

Chapter 1

What is Liberty?

If liberty is to come to our rescue, we better know what it is.

It might seem superfluous that liberty needs selling to Americans. The US Constitution opens with "We the People" establish a government to, among a very few other purposes, "Secure the Blessings of Liberty to ourselves and our Posterity." On certain occasions, we pledge our allegiance to a nation that promises "Liberty and justice for all." Liberty appears on our coins, and one of our iconic symbols is a statue honoring liberty, a gift to the United States by the people of France.

It would be natural then to expect liberty to be familiar to the great majority of citizens and that our laws would be consistent with it. That this is not the case can easily be demonstrated by querying the next ten people you meet on the street on the meaning of liberty, or by critically examining some of our major laws and widespread public opinions.

Look up liberty in a dictionary and you will find something about acting without restraint, or not being in jail. Sailors are rewarded by a day of liberty ashore in a foreign port. My thesis is that none of these ideas come close to the grand ideal held by the founders of our republic, nor do they help evaluate public policy.

1

We have a national political party, the Libertarian, with a capital L, dedicated to liberty, but this party seems unable to attract more than about ten percent of voters.

We can do better than this.

Getting the concept of liberty right is half the battle. Liberty's opponents, and there are many, will mischaracterize it and then argue that their mischaracterization would be a poor way to organize society. And they would be right.

Before trying to analyze liberty or discover its value we need a working definition. Its implications will be explored later, but let's start the discussion on a solid footing with something simple.

Liberty is usually expressed as describing the relationship between individuals and government, such as freedom of speech and religion, or fair trials. This makes it remote from daily life, and therefore out of mind. I suggest that basing the primary definition on how we restrain our own behavior clarifies its meaning. We can then extend the principle to government.

Properly defined, **liberty is the state of living with freedom of individual action under limited rules restricting your own behavior.** It defines a desirable way to live in society. This definition also implies that liberty means not being controlled or managed by someone else without your permission.

Liberty, therefore, restrains action that infringes on the freedom of others without demanding any particular action. The rules of liberty prohibit but don't mandate. In this sense, they are negative rules, but we will see they have wonderfully positive results.

Stated in an elementary personal way,[1][*] the rules of liberty are:

- I don't hit people who don't hit me.
- I don't take their stuff.
- I don't lie to them or try to trick them.
- I don't dump my garbage on their lawn.
- I don't try to force them to believe what I believe.

Liberty has been defined in more sophisticated adult ways but casting it in everyday language highlights its essential nature.

This approach follows a practice the author learned as a researcher in electrical engineering. The idea is to eliminate as many confounding factors as possible to concentrate on fundamentals.

In addition to being simple, these rules are reasonable. We probably all follow them in our personal lives, at least when we're behaving in ways that make us proud. We teach them to our children.

We will refine the rules and apply them to government as we go deeper. Some policies derived from them may raise objections at their first introduction, but the hope is that most will be allayed as the picture is developed.

Let's look at each liberty rule in a little more detail.

I don't hit people who don't hit me

Hit is shorthand for a physical attack. I expect I can be in my home or in public without serious fear of such an attack, and I will extend the same courtesy to others. But note I retain the right of self-defense. By not claiming the right to physically

---

[*] End notes are collected after the last chapter, before the index, separately numbered for each chapter. Most of them point to sources illustrating or expanding upon issues raised in the text.

attack those not attacking me I am also giving up the right to force anyone to do any particular thing. We will see this is hugely important.

Liberty doesn't assume a dreamy utopia or a new and better kind of person. I don't hit people who don't physically attack me. If someone attacks me or tries to take my stuff, I expect to need to defend myself appropriately. This applies equally to nations and individuals. There can be endless debate about what constitutes an attack or the proper response, but the principle is clear.

Physical Attack

The don't-hit rule is built around physical attack for a very good reason. Such an attack is objectively clear. A competent observer can tell if I hit someone or not. In serious cases, there is physical evidence of injury. If the definition was based on criteria such as "hurt" or simply "attack," it could be stretched to cover mere words or images. I'm not going to physically attack someone simply because he calls me a bad name.* Of course, if his speech can reasonably be interpreted as a precursor to a physical attack, such as "Give me your money or I'll kill you," a physical response that appears necessary to neutralize the threat may be appropriate.

Take schoolyard bullying for example. If a reasonable person, even a child, might interpret bullying words as threats of imminent physical attack, then an immediate physical response may be warranted. Depending on the situation though, resort to the authorities charged with enforcing the rules, such as a school principal or police officer might be more prudent.

---

* The rules of libel require that there be actual damage computable in dollars, not just hurt feelings.

Not Revenge

A refinement of the don't-hit rule requires both proportionality and immediacy. Response delayed to the point of being revenge rather than defense is not allowed, though recourse to legal process is always legitimate. This is an advance over the customs of more primitive cultures, where, for example, killing a man who utters certain disparaging remarks is justified by peculiar concepts of honor or religious orthodoxy. That this still exists in certain parts of the world, or even in subcultures in America, reminds us that liberty is not yet a universally accepted norm of behavior. The concept as developed here is barely a few hundred years old.

The don't-hit rule sounds naïve to the point of being insufficient to do much good in the real world, but it isn't. It even applies when someone has views or belongs to a political party which I abhor. I won't disrupt a public speech, no matter the subject, by making so much noise the speaker cannot be heard. This would be a form of violence calling for an appropriate and prudent response. I won't physically prevent people from entering an establishment with whose policies or practices I disagree. I may hold up a sign, but I won't hit anyone with it.

Slavery would be an extreme example of violating this and the next rule because it relies on physical force to control the life and work of another, which leads us to . . .

I don't take their stuff

This rule recognizes private property and depends on what that means. For our purposes, it is anything one creates, is freely given, or obtains by a freely entered contract from someone who legitimately owned it. It's based on the idea that the person who creates something owns it. That something can be a physical or intellectual object. It certainly includes one's labor and the person himself.

I don't claim the right to take someone's property even if I am convinced that my need for it is greater than theirs.

The need to pay taxes to support the defense of liberty is an obvious and strictly limited exception. But even here the rules are permissive because they don't restrict a person who doesn't like them from leaving that State.

An important extension is to property held in common, that is, public property. For now, let's just say I don't take public property either, at least not without following properly established rules or a specific legitimate agreement.

Information that one creates about oneself and protects by appropriate means should be considered private property. Unauthorized appropriation of such information, or property, violates liberty. This leads to customs and laws protecting privacy and one's personal space including any information created within it if that space is suitably defined and protected. I might take a photograph of someone acting foolishly in public, but not if it means peeking into his house.

The privacy aspect of liberty has become a major issue because of the need to ferret out hidden terrorists before they commit mayhem. It also comes into play when we consider regulating the desire of businesses to exploit the digital tracks individuals leave in the normal course of social and commercial transactions using modern technology.

I don't lie to them or try to trick them

Any culture, especially one as complex as ours, relies on a certain level of social trust.

I won't provide information that I know to be false to induce someone to do something that they would not do if they knew what I know. This is obviously important in commerce or trade because both parties must know what they are exchanging. Deliberate misrepresentation, or fraud, is a kind of theft.

It's tempting to say that honesty is just universally good behavior, but there are individuals, and even some subcultures, that celebrate the ability to make a "sharp" deal by withholding relevant facts. The prohibition goes beyond active fraud or lying and is a step toward a cultural advance.

I may want to make an attractive deal, but I don't want to "put something over on you." We're not talking about a poker game, where all parties know that relevant information will be withheld. Even here though, a certain degree of well-defined honesty is expected.

This rule is a two-way street requiring some degree of mutual understanding. There's nothing wrong with exchanging used or damaged goods if both parties are aware of this general fact. There's also nothing wrong with boasting if it's presented as such. "I have the best used cars in town" is not to be taken as a firm promise based on objective facts.

The same caveat applies to political speech. "I'm for the middle class" or "I will make America great again" are not the same as promising to enact a particular measure or institute a specific policy. Even here though, political speech is allowed enormous latitude. Chapters 6 and 7 will explore the question of honesty in governing at some length. But for now, let's just remember the principle.

I don't dump my garbage on their lawn

This sounds trivial, but when you think of air pollution as garbage and the air we breathe as equivalent to a lawn, it states an important principle. Liberty means not having to breathe or drink someone else's effluent, as well as not being the one who discharges it. Considering the earth is where people live, it becomes a general regard for the health of our environment.

Like any other rule, this can be distorted in its interpretation and enforcement. We'll have more to say about that later.

I don't try to force them to believe what I believe

Unlike the other rules, this one applies mostly to government because an individual violating it would need to use force, which would already violate the don't-hit rule. It is stated this way for emphasis. Neither I nor the government may <u>prevent</u> someone from expressing an idea by speech or writing. Nor may we <u>require</u> such an expression or an equivalent act.

The rule is comprehensive, but there are a few very limited exceptions prohibiting actually damaging expressions such as libel, conspiracy to commit a crime, or dealing in child pornography.

The rule applies even if I'm convinced the person's belief is wrong. But it doesn't mean every idea is equally valid or worthy of respect. Therefore, neither I nor the government may be required to provide the means for expressing a belief. The rule simply means we are certain that peaceful discourse and debate is a better way to affect beliefs than resort to physical force.

A corollary is we recognize that not every question has been adequately settled, though some very good answers exist. We want the freedom to debate openly. The United States has been almost unique in the world in this degree of liberty, yet many Americans don't realize this, much less value it. For example, we have none of the speech laws common in other countries. We'll see later these freedoms are critical for our full development as humans.

This all sounds simple and natural when stated this way, but there is always someone who will attempt to use force to prevent an idea or belief from being expressed, or to force the profession of a particular belief. In some countries, you can lose your head if you depart from the established religion.[2] In dictatorships, disciplined massed marchers must express fealty to the "leader" vocally and enthusiastically.[3]

The meaning of speech, press, and religion can be stretched beyond the applicability of this rule. Calling human sacrifice a religious practice doesn't make it anything other than murder. Screaming at someone at levels that prevent that person's opinions from being heard doesn't merit protecting the screams as speech.

Overview of Liberty

At its core, liberty is not about who has control over whom, or what rights the people or rulers have. It's more about how we control ourselves so we can live freely in a relatively peaceful society where no one is forced to do anything against his or her will. We are free, but there are no guarantees. The self-control aspect of liberty is the foundation for much of what is good about societies and governments that foster a libertarian* culture.

Liberty recognizes that people are very different in their aspirations, beliefs, needs, and abilities, and should be free to pursue these as they choose. It attempts only to limit some of their possible interactions so that each can have the benefits of maximum freedom of action without limiting that of others. There is no need to say "individual" liberty. That's the only kind there is.

While liberty is based on self-restraint, its value lies in the extent to which other people follow the same rules, which is where government comes in. We will always need laws restraining behavior that violates liberty's rules, but we must be very circumspect in making laws that require behavior.

Liberty and freedom are related, but not quite the same thing. The usual expressions of freedom focus on specific things a person may do, like speak or travel, while liberty says what most of us, including the government, will not do. Freedom exists when government observes the self-restraint of liberty.

---

* This book uses "libertarian", not capitalized, as a simple adjective meaning one who values or practices the principles or rules of liberty.

These simple rules can be expanded into much more specific laws. But for the present purpose, and to apply a test of reason to such laws, they give us a clear and solid foundation upon which to build.

Chapter 2

What Liberty is not

The opponents of liberty, either from malice or ignorance, commonly attribute a negative meaning to it, always different from the rules stated here, then attack that. Here are some examples.

Liberty is not license. Those who would replace liberty with a contrary principle commonly claim that it's just a fancy way of saying you get to do whatever you want, and to hell with everyone else, especially weaker people. The rules of liberty offered here should put this to rest.

A related objection is that liberty allows some people to gain economic power over others. While some will do better than others, and as a result may have more influence, an important responsibility of government is to prevent use of physical or legal force in doing so. Antitrust laws resist this tendency.[1] While they aren't perfect, and we can argue about details, their purpose is to maintain a fluid market in goods and services so consumers and producers have choices free of coercion. See, for example, Geoffrey Manne and Justin Hurwitz for a discussion of the difference between preventing corporate "bigness" and avoiding consumer harm.[2]

Another objection to liberty is that it has not meant the same thing throughout history, nor has it always been consistently practiced by those who preach it. Some signers of the Declaration of Independence held slaves. Few, if any, of them thought women should vote. They and many successors in government did not extend our proposed rules of liberty to the treatment of Native Americans.

These historical discrepancies from perfection do not detract from the concept. They only recognize it has developed gradually. People aren't perfect. Take the rules of liberty for what they are and try to live by them.

Opponents of liberty occasionally claim it applies only to a person living in isolation. This misses the point entirely. The rules for liberty are all about human interaction. Far from being something that was relevant only in a mythical past, liberty is a fairly recent development in the human family. The past was generally authoritarian, often based on force of arms or secret knowledge.

Liberty doesn't mean every man for himself. It in no way precludes people joining in voluntary associations, such as businesses, churches, charities, professional groups or civic associations to pursue common interests. It only denies legitimacy to compelling association by force. A later chapter will show that government should not be the first choice for pursuing common interests, especially when that commonality is less than complete.

Liberty depends on core standards of behavior. This can be a problem for those who believe that the very existence of moral, cultural or even artistic standards is objectionable. Dennis Prager argues this is because where there are standards, there is judgment, and narcissists don't want to be judged.[3]

Liberty emphatically doesn't mean no-government. It does, though, require government to be limited to carefully enumerated powers, which may be extensive. It is not about government, but government is necessary to preserve it.

Liberty is also not the answer to all of life's problems. It does not by itself *do* anything. It does, though, *enable* actions that make for a good life, many of which are impossible without liberty. It doesn't tell us how to find food, a place to live, or a mate, but it provides freedom from coercion while trying.

Liberty is sometimes depreciated as being irrelevant to a hungry person. On the contrary, a hungry person needs an environment of liberty to be free to work and enjoy the fruits of that labor. Liberty also doesn't restrict others from assisting that person. It just doesn't force that. We all need to plan and organize our lives, join or create associations, such as businesses, that support our careers, and conduct those careers ambitiously and skillfully. Liberty is simply the rules by which we exercise restraint while doing that.

To be very clear, liberty does not deny the necessity of government or its use of force. The task of the statesman is to apply the force granted by the people to preserve liberty without using it to other ends. In a single phrase, the principle of liberty is Live and Let Live, which is a version of the Golden Rule, as we will see when we briefly discuss religion in Chapter 9.

Chapter 3

The Value of Liberty

Liberty can be appreciated from personal, cultural, spiritual, and even cosmic perspectives. The personal perspective may be easiest to understand and has the most literature, so we'll start there.

A Personal Perspective

The idea that a person can live free from the arbitrary power of others has developed gradually.

Our animal and caveman ancestors lived in a hierarchy of dominance. Apparently, our brains evolved to thrive in that environment. So, it's familiar. Dominating and accepting dominance come naturally.

The ancient Greeks developed the concept of democracy; where at least some people had influence over their government. This limited and unfortunately temporary freedom wasn't close to what we would call liberty,[1] but it was a start. Conquest of Greece by Rome and later the Ottoman Empire put further development of liberty there on hold for over a thousand years.

For our purposes, we can start the history of liberty somewhere around the seventeenth century. The exact date doesn't matter. The point is that liberty is a historically recent development. It's not built into our DNA. If it were natural to humans, it would have developed long ago in prehistory, which it didn't. It's a creation of our intellect.

An early beacon illuminating some elements of liberty would be John Locke (1632–1704), a prominent English philosopher who conceptualized individual rights as natural and inalienable when these ideas were novel or even treasonous. This enlightened idea caught on, but slowly.

"Give me liberty or give me death!" is a ringing phrase at the end of a speech Patrick Henry gave in the Virginia House of Burgesses in 1775 to encourage the members to join the revolution that eventually created the United States of America. The significance of his speech in the present context is that he had to sell the idea of liberty. It existed but wasn't commonly held as a prime condition of the good life. After all, his audience had all been born, raised and prospered under the rule of a centuries-old monarchy. To our good fortune, he made the sale.

After the formation of our republic, we have Ralph Waldo Emerson (1803–1882)[2] writing "To be yourself in a world that is constantly trying to make you something else is the greatest accomplishment," emphasizing the inherent pleasure that comes from guiding your own life.

That the idea was still fairly new and undeveloped is clear from the facts that holding humans as slaves was still being debated and few thought of women participating in public life.

These pioneers understood that liberty transcends wealth, status or power. It's the satisfaction of knowing you have made your own choices creating your own life and you live in a culture where that freedom is available to all. Your choice may be to work a small farm, repair cars, live in a commune, or play a part in a large corporation, but it's yours.

You make the life you live and live the life you make. You accept the advantages and disadvantages you start with and do the best you can. You try to adopt the successful strategies you learn about from others and help them do the same.

A life well lived, according to our inner intelligence and consciousness, in other words our conscience, has its own inherent value. (This applies to adults brought to that stage of development by their parents. None of us start out ready for this). We are free to use the brain evolution has given us, and the principles of liberty that our culture has bequeathed us, to choose our path. I don't try to force others to believe as I do, and I expect the same in return.

This doesn't mean isolation. A satisfying life almost always involves living and working with others in mutually beneficial, productive and creative ways. The mutual dependence within a family or another close group seems to help. If we can share the adventure with a loving life partner, so much the better, but the main choices must be ours based on our understanding of our place and value in the river of life.

Liberty is a personal state, and not primarily about one's relation to government, though we will see later that government can limit it while being necessary to enjoy it.

A Cultural Perspective

Liberty is the only known system of social behavior that is inherently stable. This is because every other way that society has been organized depends on a hierarchy of power where some people dictate the lives and property of others, leading to inevitable conflict even among those enforcing the rules. Kings make war on each other. Nobles conspire to depose the King. The King's cousin tries to poison him. The nobles steal from the gentry and they all trample on the common folk. In the 20th century, concentration of unchecked power in nominally egalitarian governments led to the worst forms of tyranny. These are all gross violations of the principles of liberty.

There will always be those who violate liberty's rules. The self-defense principle tells us a government strong enough to control these miscreants is necessary. Constitutional control of such power is a permanent theme of maintaining liberty.

Liberty doesn't mean an absence of competition with unequal results, only that the competition must be without physical force. Differences in heritage, ambition, ideas, products, or services will lead to unequal levels of property, comfort or political influence, but force must not be part of the equation.

Humans are social beings. Living together in groups is essential to our survival. The rules of liberty make that possible while preserving our intrinsic individual essence and worth.

The distinction between individuals and groups is important because the necessity for living in groups can be corrupted to mean that the group has primacy over its members, which except in a few very special circumstances discussed later always leads to tyranny. Only an individual can feel the pain of losing liberty to a tyrant or the joy of being free to choose.

Liberty requires little of citizens beyond self-control, a simple-sounding but crucial concept developed in depth by Tom Palmer.[3] Key elements are that individuals need not fear impersonal forces backed up by armed men telling them what to do. They must only obey a few laws telling them what not to do. Our lives are our own if we mind our own business and deal fairly and civilly with others.[4] We can cooperate or not. This is the recipe for civil peace, safety, and stability.

Any system that requires obeying orders from powerful people depends on a constant balancing of large forces and is therefore unstable, or at best only conditionally stable. People must group themselves into power blocs to control these forces through the political process or worse. They must devote time and energy simply to defending their own interests or attempting to gain control over others. This unhappy condition is not limited to classical dictatorships. It can happen in democracies.

As we examine governance, we'll see several alternatives to liberty. These try to distract us by singing a siren song appealing to our desire for social perfection or personal comfort, but their reliance on coercion always leads to tyranny of one kind or another. Avoiding this is a major cultural value of liberty.

A Spiritual Perspective

Liberty can be justified on divine authority, as in "God-given rights." Or if man is believed to be created in the image of God, who certainly must be free to think His own thoughts, men and women also must be free to follow their conscience. In 1775 we find Thomas Jefferson drafting a declaration for Great Britain's American colonies, stating that

We hold these truths to be self-evident, that all men are created equal, that they are endowed by their Creator with certain unalienable Rights; that among these are Life, Liberty and the pursuit of Happiness.

This has been called "One of the best-known sentences in the English language" [5] containing "The most potent and consequential words in American history." [6] In a longer passage, it asserts its reliance on "Laws of Nature and of Nature's God."

Neither Jefferson nor his fellow signers of the Declaration of Independence (a later characterization) [7] felt compelled to define liberty or further explain the nature of the God who created all and promulgates fundamental laws. This belief in a transcendent, spiritual being was so pervasive at the time and still is for many people, that these propositions were confidently stated as being self-evident. The connection to a divine creator was, and is, a powerful justification for liberty.

Ambiguity in the meaning of "created equal" can lead to erroneous principles and dysfunctional policies. If it is interpreted to mean equal in all respects, it is obviously factually wrong. The only rational interpretation is equal in the eyes of God or the Law, with equal rights as a human being based on our spiritual connection to the creator.

One of the remarkable aspects of liberty is that it comfortably encompasses a basis in the moral universes of both believers and non-believers. No other system of political philosophy comes close to this degree of inclusiveness. The next section is a blazing example of this universality.

A Cosmic Perspective

This is a relatively new way to approach the value of liberty, without a well-developed literature, so we'll examine it in more detail than for the more traditional avenues. We will discover a new way liberty uniquely enhances and supports an expanded concept of human life. While not a new conclusion, this is so important that taking the time to put it on a firm objective foundation is worth the effort because liberty is far from universally accepted or even appreciated. It needs all the support it can get.

Taking a fresh look at the value of liberty is not to say that previous defenses were wrong or poorly founded. They were groundbreaking when originally developed, have served well since, and are still valid. But it never hurts to re-examine our fundamental beliefs if for no other reason than to gain new and greater appreciation for them.

The vast increases in power appropriated by all levels of government suggest that the debate about liberty, including even what it means, is not over. So, let's start from scratch and see if we can improve the discussion.

A Foundation for Ethics

The basic questions then are—why is liberty good? What are the criteria for choosing one form of government over another? What does *good* even mean in this context?

To answer these questions, we need to develop a foundation for ethics and a philosophical basis for making political judgments. Critics may argue that they are pragmatic or moderate and simply judge policy by whether it is "good" or it "works" without relying on philosophy. But that is a false argument because all such judgments are based on an internal philosophy whether one holds that philosophical basis consciously or not.

The issue here is political order, not personal philosophy like why I love someone or prefer one symphony over another.

In the public realm, unlike in personal life, one must at least discuss, if not convince others of, one's proposals for policy. The bases or premises for judging the value of various goods[*] must be clear and amenable to objective critique based on facts and clear principles. Policy based on simple assertions, no matter how ancient, authoritative, or superficially appealing, rests on raw power, caprice, or deception.

The need for clarity is evident from the fact that while most American politicians nominally profess our founding principles as expressed in the Declaration of Independence and Constitution, their application of these principles can lead to diametrically opposite types of laws. They lack clarity in the concepts and premises behind their sentiments. We can do better, so let's dig deeper.

Start at the Beginning

How far back in the logical chain of abstract principles supporting more directly applicable ones must we go to find a bedrock objective truth to support an edifice of public ethics and morality? Let's start with existence. To do this effectively we take a short tour through cosmology and evolution.

---

[*] In this context, any desirable thing or condition is a <u>good</u>. That's not an adjective; it's a noun that isn't limited to things you buy in a store.

The fundamental objective fact is the existence of the universe. We, through science, know a lot, but certainly not everything, about that.

One of the most significant facts we've learned about the universe in the last century, well after developing the basic ideas of liberty and governance, is that it both evolves and undergoes major changes in its nature.

Emergences

We call these big changes *emergences*.[8] The universe becomes different in kind, not just bigger or older. The terms evolution and emergence seem justified by the fact that over its history the universe has done much more than simply change in a linear way. [9, 10] This doesn't imply a plan or a mechanism such as the DNA that maintains the pattern of life's evolution, but it implies a process, which we're starting to learn. As far as we know, the universe evolves following physical laws which we know remarkably well, yet profoundly imperfectly.

We have an immense advantage over previous philosophers here, not because we're smarter, we're just better informed. We're standing on the shoulders of giants like Einstein, Hubble, Bohr, Heisenberg and many others.

The Big Bang

The process begins with the Big Bang. It's still a mystery how that started or where it came from, but it happened, and a long time ago. If you wish, you can say God did it.

But we do know a surprising amount about what happened immediately after the Big Bang. Leaving out volumes of detail, some of the first things we know about are quarks, which no longer exist independently, and electrons and photons, which still do. There was no mass or material or atoms as we know them because of the incredible heat energy. In just the first few seconds though, the quarks cooled a bit and coalesced into protons.

As you may recall from chemistry class, protons now form the nucleus of atoms, but it was still too hot for atoms to exist. Even so, this was a huge change in the nature of the universe, and it gets the story going.

Following that first major change in the nature of matter, after about 300 thousand years, the universe cooled enough that free-floating electrons became attached to these protons to form hydrogen atoms, most of which still exist. This was another complete transition in the nature of the universe.

After some additional time, gravity pulled together huge numbers of hydrogen atoms to form stars that burn with their own light. This is not burning in the familiar sense, but fusing together of hydrogen into progressively heavier elements, because of the gravitational pressure of their combined mass, which releases energy. The heavier elements are later spewed into space by stellar pressure. The creation of stars that create heavier elements was another change so significant that it must count as an emergence, or step in cosmic evolution.

Even more spectacularly, stars somewhat larger than our Sun eventually explode as a supernova, creating all the heavy elements—carbon, nitrogen, potassium, iron, gold—the entire periodic table.

These elemental heavy atoms spent a long time floating around in space, but over time gravity also clumped them together to form planets, like ours.

This sequence, or process, must qualify as something more than just linear change. Emergence seems a fitting descriptor for these examples of magnificent steps in creation. And now, thanks to some gross simplifications, that's all we need from cosmology.

Be patient. We're on track to see some equally significant and more familiar emergences in the evolution of living things.*

Life
On our planet, life emerged. It also might have emerged on other planets. We don't know. At least it's here.

In the living world, emergences happen gradually and can be recognized only after many tiny steps, but they are remarkable once developed and distinct from their antecedents.

Though the mechanism is still obscure to us (there are several plausible possibilities[11]), the emergence of life itself from inanimate material is by any standard a profound example of a major emergence.

Other more clearly understood emergences are the creation of cells having an inside and an outside, multicellular creatures and plants, creatures with a nervous system, and mammals. All living creatures are constructed of the material of our planet, and therefore of the universe.

There is no need to attribute a purpose to this evolution. It just seems to be the way the universe works. Anyone who claims there is a purpose is guessing. As with cosmology itself, here again, we have the advantage of standing on the shoulders of giants such as Darwin, Mendel, R. Franklin, Watson, and Crick.

Humans
Eventually, life produces humans, who from early days have been conscious of much more than their immediate surroundings. They tell stories of what's on the other side of a distant mountain, or what happened several generations ago. Or even what might happen next year. At some point, they speculate about and then carefully observe the planets and stars.

---

* Emergence as used here is a well-understood description of natural processes not to be confused with the same term used to suggest externally planned and directed steps in evolution.

They (we) are becoming conscious of the rest of the universe.

Cosmic Self Consciousness

But we are a part of the universe, so <u>the universe is becoming conscious of itself</u>.

This, I submit, has to be one of the most significant emergences of all time. Think of it. A universe that has been around at least thirteen billion years has in the last few thousand years started to become conscious of itself.

Earth not only developed life, which is a big enough emergence on its own, but this life eventually became conscious of its history and cosmic surroundings. This is a huge emergence, and so important that it's worth restating.

We humans are not detached observers contemplating the universe. We are the part of the universe conscious of the whole, or at least the part we know about. We are, as far as we know, the first creatures to be aware of our evolution as part of the universe, to study its mechanisms, and possibly to direct, or at least affect it.

This, I contend, gives humans a unique and significant status among all creatures and material beings.

Human Role in the Cosmos

Stewardship

Before delving too deeply into ethics as they relate to human relations, we need briefly to consider that conferring primacy on humans could lead us to forget that Earth is where we live. Primacy doesn't mean dominance. It's more like stewardship. The earth must survive and support our evolution for us to play our part in the cosmic saga. Since we don't know exactly what support we need for that evolution, we should be mindful of what we do know about the earth, including the interactions of its parts, and choose actions responsibly.

In this context, *responsibly* means doing nothing likely to materially impair our ability, representing the consciousness of the universe, to further develop that consciousness and understanding.

This implies a due, not absolute, regard for our environment. For example, we and the snail darter[12] (an unremarkable little fish) do not have equal existential standing. It means it is up to us to decide how to live with the snail darter, not the other way around. We should not ignore the snail darter, but its significance lies in how it indicates the health of the general biosphere in which we live. We must be conscious that we don't know everything, but we can still make judgments based on what we know or can discover about a particular case.

Similarly, since other humans carry the remainder of our cosmic consciousness, we must be mindful of, not slavishly subservient to, their survival and well-being.

With the foregoing as a foundation, we can develop higher-level principles including ethics.

Life Planning

One of the principal aims of philosophy is to determine the nature of the *good*. That is, what might be the desirable ends, or purpose, of life? This is most relevant to human life because humans must choose how to live. If this isn't obvious, consider that all the other animals manage to live just fine by running mostly on instinct, that is, patterns of behavior built into their DNA by a long process of natural selection. Even when they incorporate learned behavior into their lives, as when mother wolves teach their cubs how to hunt, engaging in this process is itself an instinctual act. As far as we know, young wolves do not start their adult lives thinking something like, "Should I become a hunter like mom and dad or maybe a musician and howl beautifully all day?" Wolves don't consciously decide to have pups. They certainly don't question the morality of eating other creatures.

This necessity for humans to make major life choices requiring long-term planning and commitment represents enough of a difference between us and the other animals to be considered a major emergence. Examples include educational preparation years before needing to earn a living or preparing for life after the best earning years. Just because some humans don't succeed well at this doesn't diminish its importance to our evolutionary path.

To develop a concept of the good, it's helpful to recall we are not only a part of the universe and its evolution but are on a leading edge of that evolution because of the breadth and nature of our consciousness. The nature of evolution seems to be toward more complexity, and in our case, toward a more complete consciousness and understanding of evolution itself and the universe in which it occurs. It seems then that fostering this evolution, or at least not impeding it, must be good. We also must remember there is no reason to believe evolution has stopped.

Since humans carry the consciousness of the universe, another aspect of the good must be to support and foster us in our performance of this activity. That is, the life of humans as thinking, choosing beings is good in itself. This is not to imply that humans in general or even specific ones are perfect — far from it. But as far as we know, we carry the most consciousness of the universe and its history of anyone in our galactic vicinity. We might as well proceed on this basis until contrary evidence is available.

Remember "Carrying the consciousness of the universe" means the universe being conscious of itself, not that we are something separate being conscious of a universe distinct from ourselves. This seems to impose a significant responsibility on us humans.

What are some implications of assigning the status of a primary good to a person's life as a thinking rational being?

Freedom to Think and Act

We must be free to think and then to act on our thought, with due regard for our role in the universe. Freedom means never having to ask permission for thoughts. Nor for actions that neither infringe on the freedom of others nor impede the progress of human evolution. Another word for this is liberty.

Human creative thinking is always done by individuals. It may be stimulated by working in a group. Or, an idea may be distributed by groups, and other individuals may improve it, but every original idea comes from one person. The consequence of this is that the value of liberty accrues to individuals. Naturally, when people live in groups whose members all enjoy some benefit, the group can be said to do the same, just as they would all be cold in a snowstorm. But only individuals feel that cold or enjoy liberty.

A person must know he is responsible for the rational choices and follow through that will support his life. Freedom is not synonymous with success. It is simply the freedom to try. We must be responsible for our life because if we are not, we abrogate our rationality to someone else, and we may as well not exist. If we do not exercise our ability to choose rationally, then we are acting simply as instinctive animals; which denies our nature. Worse yet would be to act as a domestic animal, like cattle. The nature of humans is fundamentally different from that of cattle, which exist to benefit the rancher. Their lives may seem contented, but they are not independent actors. Humans, however, exist for their own benefit. If they are forced or choose to exist for the benefit of someone else, they are being treated like or acting like cattle. A more familiar example might be acting or being treated like children. The argument is the same.

It should be obvious that man's life is a primary good because if he does not survive, then he cannot contribute to evolution. These observations suggest that fostering human rationality and the ability to think long term should be a goal of any system of ethics or morality that organizes public life. The rules of liberty attempt to achieve this.

Evolution and Liberty

Our emphasis has been on the consciousness of the universe, acting in us, being a primary good. No special choosing by humans beyond avoiding impeding this process is implied. It's possible to speculate that a new emergence may be the development of the necessity to make choices about the direction of evolution. This is probably premature. Simply protecting our little part of the universe and its natural evolution is proving difficult enough. Making active choices will be harder and will require the evolution of even greater human intelligence and wisdom. The evolutionary process got us here, so it must be good in itself. Let's not screw it up.

Rules for a life well lived have been known for a long time. Having the leisure and knowledge to examine the implications of cosmic consciousness is an added, precious gift. One way to use this gift is to employ our human rationality to the best of our ability. Be rational. Think on a large scale and long term. Practice the rules of liberty. They most emphatically don't tell us what to do or what to think, but they are guidelines for how to behave while we're doing that.

Beyond this, I don't pretend to know exactly how to use this consciousness. But realizing that I'm part of a majestic emergence on a cosmic scale brings a sense of wonder, gratitude, and responsibility.

Chapter 4

Governing for Liberty

Government is not the enemy of liberty.
It must be strong enough to defend liberty, but not allowed to destroy it.

Liberty is appealing from several perspectives. Everyone should be for it. Isn't that enough?

No. We need government to protect us from those individuals and nations that chose not to live by liberty's rules. Even their seemingly intuitive truth does not make them natural or self-enforcing — far from it. In turn, government needs liberty to ensure a long, stable existence. This interdependence condemns liberty and government to an eternal marriage. We must understand how that marriage can be made to work.

The essence of liberty is to live and let live according to the rules of self-control. Individual force is justified only in the rare event of self-defense. Most interactions between free people are conducted in *civil society*, the complex web of voluntary arrangements by which people live, work, and play in the social space between family and government.

The essence of government, in contrast, is the use of force to prevent, punish, or coerce action. Reconciling these opposing natures is the key to designing and maintaining a legitimate government. Building roads and other infrastructure, setting standards for weights and measures, creating a common currency and providing other public goods are natural uses for government power, but preserving liberty is necessarily the primary objective. If government fails in that, it doesn't matter how good the roads are because the people will be in constant fear of assault, theft, or other attack.

Let us examine the relationship between liberty and government in more detail, starting with a brief review of how governments and liberty evolved. We can then move on to the constitution that defines our government and how that government fulfills its responsibilities.

Evolution of Government

Liberty is not a natural state of human society. If it were, it would have been established as the norm for governance millennia ago. It's a recent emergence in the long pathway of evolution, and like most, it starts locally and small. It's not a natural extension of communal and hierarchical prehistoric tribal society, and certainly not of feudalism. While the liberal western tradition, both classically and as developed here, considers liberty to be an inherent human right, that view has gained traction only over time. By historical standards, it's relatively new at only a few hundred years old. It's established in only a few places in the world, and only partially there.

Liberty may not be necessary or even appropriate in small subsistence groups bound by kinship, but it becomes so in large groups whose members don't know or relate to most of the others. It must be understood in the context of complex interactions among large numbers of people. In such groups immediate face-to-face sanction cannot enforce norms of behavior, thus formal rules and government evolve to keep the peace.

Governments have existed in one form or another since people lived in nations rather than tribes. Conquerors, defenders, or their descendants enforced rules for everyone else while freely violating them themselves. Without delving into the details of the evolution of political order (read Francis Fukuyama[1] for that) I think it's fair to say that one of the great cultural emergences was people themselves creating governments that depended on their consent and were also subject to rules. Governments didn't start that way. They have gained legitimacy by slowly devolving power to those being governed. The people gradually codified the rules of liberty and slowly gained control of the power necessary to enforce them.

Early Steps in Popular Control

Early steps in people gaining control over their governance appeared when German towns of the tenth century were granted limited autonomy by local kings. (There was no Germany.)[2] We see other glimmers of liberty in the demands his barons imposed on King John of England at Runnymede, near Windsor on June 15, 1215, in the *Magna Carta Libertatum*,[3] which is medieval Latin for "The Great Charter of the Liberties." These were only hints at the liberty understood in our time, but they were a start.

Liberty as an Inherent Right

In both examples, limited liberties were granted by rulers to certain subjects as partial freedom from royal or other rule. The modern understanding though is that liberty is an inherent right.

Government does not grant liberty, it protects it. Aspects of liberty such as freedom of speech or self-defense are affirmed in our constitution, but they are not granted by it or any government. Laws specify the elements of a crime against liberty, such as assault or theft, but this is only to regulate the response to such an act, which is wrong even in the absence of a specific law.

Constitutional or statutory affirmations of liberty are not to be parsed to constrain their boundaries, much less repeal or abridge them. Liberty must be understood as a basic principle, not just words in a document. This matter is discussed further in the next chapter.

The United States government was established by and derives its legitimacy from the people themselves as a unique complete break with a king. An entirely new sovereign state was formed, not a negotiated settlement of limited rights. The founders of our republic didn't ask for liberty, they took it. The agreement that creates and defines our federal government (The US Constitution) opens with:

We the People of the United States, in Order to form a more perfect Union, establish Justice, insure domestic Tranquility, provide for the common defense, promote the general Welfare, and secure the Blessings of Liberty to ourselves and our Posterity, do ordain and establish this Constitution for the United States of America.

The significant point here is that we the people establish our government. No one does it for us, and we don't receive it from anyone. It's our creation. These words aren't just boilerplate. They create the purpose of our federal government. Unlike the End User License Agreement (EULA) for which you click ACCEPT every time you open a new Twitter account, this is important to read and understand. It isn't hard but does take some thought.

Securing the blessings of liberty is one of the primary purposes of the United States Government. Each state has its own constitution with similar, but broader (plenary) objectives. That this idea has not found acceptance around the world is hardly a revelation. The United States can take pride in advancing it, even though we have not perfected it ourselves. There is no guarantee of its future perfection or even existence, which is up to us.

So, what's needed to acquire and preserve liberty?

Conditions for Liberty

The first requirement is that enough people want it. More specifically, the great majority of people must want it. For that to occur, they need to know what it is, and why it's valuable. The usual path for development of liberty is when common people and great thinkers living under tyranny, that is, lack of liberty, imagine what a more liberal life would be like and fight literally or figuratively to achieve it. With luck, they succeed in incrementally increasing their liberty, but tragically often exchange one tyranny for another. Cautionary tales include the French revolution in 1789, Russia after 1917, and Cuba since 1959. In each case, life for some was improved in some way, but liberty eluded them.

Some discover liberty's value the hard way, by being denied its blessings and suffering its absence. Most Americans are fortunate to have been born where liberty is at least partially the norm.

But when people grow up in an environment of even partial liberty along with a comfortable life, they take it for granted. They may have a superficial education in its history, but its value to them can be tarnished by neglect and failure to understand it. They can fall prey to demagogues peddling dreams of utopia. The more comfortable they are the more important is continuous education about liberty.

The value of liberty can also be forgotten because by itself it doesn't provide the necessities of life. Work does that. People in poverty for whom the most pressing issue is the next meal or a place to sleep may seek solace in promises of food and other necessities. Liberty is not even considered. Some may just want "their share". Thoughts of liberty are not a high priority, but perhaps should be if the lack of liberty thwarts a person's efforts to make a living.

The task of the libertarian is to remove government obstacles to self-improvement and free markets, and then provide education and possibly personal assistance in understanding, appreciating and participating in them. This book and many others attempt to reinforce this aspect of education.

Broad, not Absolute, Acceptance

Assuming that most people want liberty (a big assumption) we must recognize there will never be universal agreement on that. There will always be individuals and nations who believe they can improve their situation by violating the rules of liberty. Any principle for political organization that requires universal acceptance is doomed to fail. Marx and Lenin knew they needed to create a "New Soviet Man." They tried, but it didn't work.

Government is how the broad majority impose the rules of liberty on the presumably small minority who flout them. For there to be broad acceptance, the rules must be simple prohibitions of commonly despised acts, not commands to do specific things or act in specific ways. The rules of liberty don't define the culture or what people do, only what they may not do.

A liberal government is a tool the people create and control for a purpose. It, therefore, cannot be the same thing as the people who create it. This is often confused by statements such as "The government is what we all do together." It isn't what we all do together; it's a tool we use to enforce what the great majority of us agree not to do to each other. President Lincoln's famous statement in the Gettysburg Address is often misinterpreted. "Of, by, and for the people" mean that the government is created by the people, its members come from, that is they are of the people, and its purpose is for the people. His statement doesn't mean that the government is the people or that the people are the government. These distortions lead to consequences fatal to liberty, as we will see in later sections. Lincoln, in his concise poetic prose, didn't need to make such distinctions because at that time the federal government was not nearly as pervasive as it is now.

Great Power of Limited Scope

A government that's intended to defend liberty must be more powerful than any threat. It must have secret intelligence capability and military might to discover and disable serious threats before they kill millions of us. It must detect and punish sophisticated domestic and international crime. It will be a powerful machine, like a bulldozer, and therefore dangerous. A bulldozer is useful, even essential for some jobs, but it's not our friend, much less our mother. It's a tool for a purpose.

Advocates for a particular cause are drawn to federal power because it is so great and extends over the entire country. If enacted into federal law, their cause is much harder to escape than if it were enacted only by states or was not enshrined in law at all. We often hear that some "problem" is not being "adequately addressed" by civil society or states, so the federal government "must" take charge. This violates the liberty rule of not forcing others to believe as I do even if I'm convinced they're wrong.

This was recognized by Henry Kissinger in his 1954 book on making peace after the Napoleonic wars. "The most fundamental problem of politics ... is not the control of wickedness but the limitation of righteousness." [4]

One protection against this danger is to restrict government authority to appropriate nationwide, statewide, or local issues. Consider the federal government, which in promoting the general welfare logically has a role in issues such as public safety, clean air, and roads. Federal reach must, though, be restricted to only those issues inherently national or at least regional (multi-state) in nature, not just extent. For example, air pollution or a criminal syndicate that extends over a multi-state area is inherently national because the sources, victims, and mechanisms themselves are causally and often diffusely connected over different states or even larger regions.

Obesity, in contrast, may exist nationwide but is inherently personal. Scientifically studying its causes and providing information about its effects could legitimately be considered national in character supporting the general welfare. It would even be legitimate for a president, or president's spouse, to use the prominence of the office to informally popularize good dietary habits. But legislatively regulating the food intake of individuals should not be an issue for national, statewide or even local government.[5] It would be if citizens were thought to be resources of the State, and the health of the State was a primary objective, as in having strong soldiers, but we aren't, and it isn't.

The liberty rule that states I won't try to force others to believe as I do can be made more concrete. Specifically, and when possible, laws should recognize the differences in beliefs and standards in different states or even communities by being enacted only by the lowest level of government that effectively encompasses the issue at hand. Local laws must, though, adhere to the basic rules of liberty because those define our nation.

Governing vs. Managing

Governing differs from managing. A manager's task is to cause subordinates to believe what he or she believes about goals, objectives, and methods. Good management is needed in an organization but not at the point of a gun in a free society. Government is good at preventing people from harming each other. It's not very good at forcing them to cooperate, or even be nice to each other. Doing so would violate the liberty rule of not forcing others to believe as I do.

We need to be governed, but we don't need to be managed. Liberty properly limits what we do to others, but it doesn't suggest how we live our own lives. Most of us most of the time should be able to consider government policies from a detached viewpoint focusing on general welfare rather than our personal situation. Something similar was expressed more poetically by John Kennedy at his 1961 inauguration as the 35th president of the United States. "And so, my fellow Americans: ask not what your country can do for you; ask what you can do for your country." [6]

This isn't just idle philosophical speculation.

Government is not your Mother

We must try to maintain an arms-length, detached and objective relationship with government. This means limiting its impact on our personal lives so we and it can focus attention on major issues of broad national import.

Untangling government, especially at the federal level, from its intimacy with individuals can be approached by recognizing it has assumed powers well beyond those granted by the Constitution. Government can legitimately exercise only powers granted by the people through a constitution, and the people can logically grant only powers they themselves possess.

As a concrete example, I can delegate some of my right of self-defense to a government. But I can't delegate a right to take someone's property because I don't have that right in the first place. The same goes for forcing another person to believe what I believe. We'll dig deeper into this in a later section.

Overload

Another reason to restrict the scope of government is we want it to work well where it is needed. The more it takes on less legitimate responsibilities the less respect it will have, the more its leaders will lose focus, the more its resources will be diluted and the less effective it will be in those areas where it has critical responsibility.

Loss of respect is measured in polls as public confidence in government, which recently has been running only around 20%, with many important civil society enterprises, such as the press, faring little better.[7] This is inevitable when we consider the great variety of human desires, outlooks on life, and approaches to everything.

Any government policy or program will be disagreeable to some citizens and so will arouse them to object. Even though each policy may offend only a small number, if there are enough different policies, eventually everyone will have a reason to distrust or lose respect for the government. It then becomes illegitimate and must resort to force to retain any power at all.

Loss of respect, and therefore legitimacy, happens even faster when a policy is rammed through a legislature with only a slim partisan majority. This guarantees a large body of disgruntled citizens. The current battle may be won but at the cost of losing widespread support for that policy and for government itself.

Government should not be the whole story. Even though government has responsibilities beyond protecting liberty, there need not be a law for everything. Government's proper role in regulating behavior is to enforce the restrictive rules of liberty, not to command positive good behavior in general. Broccoli and kale are known to be good for you but eating them must not be required. We exhibit and enforce admirable attributes such as cooperation, generosity, kindness, and politeness by example and sometimes approbation, but without government involvement.

We are reminded of the craftsman who knows not to use a knife as a pry bar. It won't do that very well and will probably be damaged so it's no longer even a good knife. Take good care of your tools and your government. Don't wear them out.

This is the basis for suggesting that government must observe the rules of liberty to survive, just as the citizens need government to protect their own liberty. Government needs to be a good citizen. It shouldn't try to force people to believe any particular thing. Leave beliefs, and decisions based on beliefs, to the people.

Temptations of Power

The enemy of liberty is the idea that society, including its economy, is a unitary system that can be understood well enough to centrally control its most significant factors for desirable ends. Society and its economy are better understood as self-organizing systems not only needing no central direction, but suffering when it is applied. Self-organizing systems, in a nutshell, are those in which many parts each follow local rules, which don't even have to be the same, resulting in an unplanned but beneficial result.

Government, in contrast, is not self-organizing. It is a tool created with a purpose and to a plan. It is necessarily hierarchical because its purpose is to enforce rules uniformly. It has an army that must be led by a central command. It is not a good model for society. At its best, it conforms to a written constitution that limits its powers to only those required to preserve liberty and a few other well-defined objectives. At its worst, government can become an instrument of tyranny.

The unique power of government, at all levels, makes it a tempting tool by which avaricious individuals or associations attempt to deny economic liberty to potential competitors, suppliers or customers. Examples would include licensing laws that impose barriers to entry not justified by health or safety aspects of the general welfare or import restrictions with the principal effect of protecting domestic suppliers at the expense of consumers. These all have in common the use of government force to take someone's actual or potential property, which violates the rules of liberty. An example of resistance to this tendency is The Institute for Justice whose pro-bono lawyers fight legal battles to create precedents defending individuals from unnecessary restrictions on their choice of work.[8]

The final arguments for a limited, not weak, government are that the leaders may be wrong, and the only certain result of a grand new policy is unintended consequences. As essayist Jonah

Goldberg[9] put it, "In politics, the worry is very often not that the government will knowingly do wrong but that it will take the shortest path to doing what it thinks is right."

Prudence suggests that policy adjustments be made small and infrequently enough that people have time to adapt to them, and the damage from errors can be corrected at small cost.

An analogy from agriculture is apt. We have learned over the past half-century that massive farms growing only a single crop (monoculture) can be subject to disastrous disease requiring heavy use of pesticides. Such problems are less likely to occur on farms based on more diverse crops, or at least losses to a single crop are tempered by the diversity of produce to sell.

The lesson here is that forcing everyone to do the same thing at the same time is likely to go badly.

Chapter 5

The Constitution

It's no accident that the foregoing discussion of liberty and government parallels the US Constitution.

Why do we need a constitution? Why don't we just have laws, or even just a powerful president?

Liberty needs a strong government to protect it, but that strength can be hazardous to liberty. Government, therefore, must be designed carefully so it can be effective without becoming a threat.

An Exceptional Constitution

In 1787 each of the recently liberated colonies had its own government. They had fought the war of independence as a loose confederation[1] and became independent sovereign States by virtue of the treaty ending the war in 1783. Now they were countries like any other. The State of Virginia was, for example, legally on a par with the States of France or Spain. It wasn't a subdivision of anything. It was sovereign.

A short digression is in order to clarify the meanings of *state* and *sovereign*.

43

States and states

Americans are understandably uncertain about the meaning of *state*. We grow up knowing we live in a state — for example, Oregon or Virginia. We also learn that our home state is part of the United States of America and that each state is subdivided into counties. Because of this symmetry, it is easy for those not giving much thought to the matter to believe that the relation of one of our states to the federal government is the same as that of a county to its state. There appears to be a hierarchy with the smaller units being subsidiary to the larger, from cities to counties to states to the US federal government. This is essentially wrong, starting with an erroneous understanding of *state* as a subdivision of a nation.

Correctly understood, a State (often capitalized when used in this sense) is the "supreme public power within a sovereign political entity" [2] where *sovereign* means independent and supreme. The supremacy of a State is effectuated by its exercise of the *police power*, which is "the regulation and control of the affairs of a community, especially with respect to the maintenance of order, law, health, morals, safety and other matters affecting general welfare."

We'll soon see how our use of *state* has a different meaning, but returning to the post-revolutionary period, we have these now independent States retaining the loose confederation by which they had waged the war of independence.   That confederation, though, was proving incapable of resolving conflicts between them or defending their common interests. It also could not raise much revenue. They realized they needed something more to survive.

From Confederation to Union

They knew they didn't want a king, or a too-powerful central government.

So, they did two things that as far as I know were and are still exceptional, if not unique, in history.

First, the army, which was as real as that of any victorious revolutionaries, had disbanded. Unlike after most revolutions, the victorious army commanders didn't simply declare themselves to be the new government. They went home to their original States, which already existed and were now sovereign over their territories. They went back to farming, or whatever they had done before the revolution.

But then, in 1788[3], after a few years of trying to manage with their confederation, they did the second exceptional thing. They created a jointly sovereign, separate government essentially in parallel to those of their home States. They gave some, but by no means all their sovereignty to the new federal government that was to be created by the proposed constitution. The original thirteen States retained, they were not granted, the remainder of their sovereignty.

The states added since then have the same arrangement. Three later states, Texas, California and Hawaii, joined the union in a manner like the original thirteen. They were already sovereign States, some for only a short time, but they relinquished some of that sovereignty to join the Union. The rest, like Oregon, were created this way from the beginning.[*]

The important point is our states (lower case now) have all the power inherent in independent countries, except what is specifically given to the federal government by the Constitution.

This was novel and is still being worked out. Divided sovereignty was severely tested in 1861 when eleven southern states exceeded their retained sovereignty by seceding from the union. This issue was settled, at least partially, by the Civil War.

---

[*] This is not to ignore Florida, but its history and admission were too complicated to describe here. The result is the same.

Other national governments have partially self-governing subdivisions, like the Departments in France, the Autonomous Regions of Spain, and the Swiss Cantons, but these derive their authority from the central government. Scotland may be a recent partial exception in the United Kingdom, but this is evolving. The Spanish government recently removed the governor of Catalonia for holding an unauthorized election.

What's important is that our states don't receive their authority from the federal government or even the Constitution. They have it because they are sovereign in important respects.

Divided Sovereignty

The Constitution attempts to preserve liberty in part by granting the federal government those powers, and only those powers, necessary to carry out specific functions. This is stated explicitly in the Tenth Amendment,[4] the final one in the Bill of Rights:

The powers not delegated to the United States by the Constitution, nor prohibited by it to the States, are reserved to the States respectively, or to the people.

This key fact distinguishes the United States of America from, I believe, every other nation. Our states retain all sovereign powers except for those given up to the federal, not national, government which is supreme only where it has been granted enumerated powers.[5] This is not the place for a deep study of constitutional law, but important elements are that the federal government does not have the *plenary*, that is, complete, police power[*] of the states. The federal structure itself preserves the identity and a measure of equal influence of the states, despite differences in their size or population. Our government is not a democracy but something between that and a simple federation of States.

---

[*] But the Federal Government does have police power in those subjects where it is granted enumerated powers, and in the District of Columbia.

The federal government is, though, given great power to defend the nation, regulate relations between the states, conduct all international relations, establish rules for citizenship, and perform certain public services of a national nature, like build interstate roads. It can levy taxes to support these powers.

Where it's granted these authorities, it is given supreme power over the states. This is important because the authors realized that the voluntary nature of the Articles of Confederation left these independent States free to opt out of or ignore acts of the Continental Congress. They knew that the new nation needed to be able to speak and act as a single entity especially in foreign affairs and civil rights.

Police Power

Plenary police power, though, remains with, it's not granted to, the states because they were and still are sovereign in that respect. Such power is the hallmark, or definition, of a sovereign State. By ratifying the US Constitution, the people, acting through their States, gave some of that sovereignty to the federal government, but retained the rest in their states, whose sovereignty is complete with only specific limitations.

In a constitutional context, *police power* means a great deal more than just a police department. Our states can make any law they deem proper to protect the health, morals, or welfare of their citizens. This power is limited only by the US Constitution, or any self-imposed restrictions in their own constitutions. For example, our states have the inherent right to impose taxes of any kind to support these functions.

The states can define and punish crimes such as burglary, disturbing the peace, public nuisance, and fraud. They can define and punish murder. They can and do have different laws regarding such issues as marriage, inheritance, and land use. They can create public schools.

The federal government is not given the power to do any of these things. (There are special cases like crimes committed on some federal property.)

Our states can make their laws conform to those of other states, but they don't have to. They can be different so long as they don't violate constitutional protections of basic civil rights or do a very few other prohibited things like make treaties with foreign governments.

The separation of power between federal and state governments follows the liberty rule that I won't try to make others believe as I do. If the people of a state reach a suitable consensus about something like education, they can do that differently from what is done in other states. They can make it a crime to sell or smoke marijuana. But they don't have to.

The federal government is not granted such a power. Oh, wait a minute—it does it anyway. This violation of constitutional text and principles was a dereliction of duty by both federal officials and the voting public in the first half of the 20th Century. Nobody's perfect.

Separation of Powers

The very structure of the federal government created by the Constitution is or should be a defense of liberty. Power is shared by three separate branches, with none supposedly able to both enact and enforce laws. Congress itself is divided into two houses, both of which must approve new laws. Then, in another check, the president must also approve them unless both houses are almost unanimous. This makes enacting laws a slow process, which potentially defends liberty, but it also puts the same constraint on repealing laws that turn out to offend liberty.

Personal Value of State Identity

Besides these matters of political philosophy, there are profound personal values to our federal system. One of the main ones is that our people have an almost costless ability to move between states having sometimes significantly different public policies and civil societies while retaining the protections of the US government and Constitution. This is because our states retain not only important elements of sovereignty but their own identities. While each state may do things differently, within broad constitutional limits, we are reluctant to be dogmatic about which is superior.

Enumerated Powers

Except in its preamble, the US Constitution isn't aspirational. It doesn't promise anything tangible or go into any detail about what the people who wrote and ratified it hoped to achieve. Constitutions that make specific promises usually disappoint.

The Constitution is, though, clear about granting powers to the federal government and allocating them between it and the States, sometimes granting and limiting, sometimes denying. It emphasizes that the federal government is to have only specific enumerated powers and is not to be all powerful. It is not granted power simply to do "good." The purpose of restricting the federal government to specified, enumerated powers is to prevent it from dominating the states and the people.

The actual powers granted to the federal government are enumerated in Article I, Section 8. They include national defense, regulating interstate commerce, coining money, a postal service, naturalization and others. They don't include plenary police power.[6] *

The tenth amendment and inclusion of several specific (enumerated) powers make it very clear that the federal government is granted only those powers. Contrary to what may

---

* Inclusion of "provide for the . . . general welfare" in the power to tax is not a catch all making all the other grants redundant. Those are the real grants of power.

be claimed by advocates of expansive federal power, the General Welfare clause in both the preamble and section 8 of Article I can logically be read only as an objective, not as an unlimited power specifically granted. Any other interpretation would grant jurisdiction over every aspect of life, rendering the enumeration of powers superfluous. Any federal legislation not violating a specific prohibition would be acceptable. This is nonsense even if proffered by learned jurists. Misunderstanding this distinction has led to innumerable laws infringing on liberty.

Still Relevant

There is also a perennial objection that the Constitution is obsolete. It was written over two hundred years ago when there were only about 1% as many people here; those people traveled by horse and carriage; guns shot round balls with hand-loaded black powder, and there were no telephones. Perhaps it's no more than a guide to some of the mechanics of governing, like setting rules for elections and shaping the Congress. It defines who commands the army but doesn't speak of medical care or income inequality.

Maybe it isn't up to dealing with the world as it is now. Perhaps we should just forget the enumerated powers. Allow the federal government to act as though it was granted power to do whatever is "necessary" for the "common good." It would be The Government, the whole government. The states would be useful administrative subdivisions, historical artifacts without independent identity or power.

Kinds of (Federal) Power

The more we study the Constitution, though, the more we see the foresight of its authors. Even though they had no inkling of the coming changes in population, technology, or the economy, they understood people and power.

In my opinion, they established principles of governance perfectly able to continue to serve our needs and protect our liberty. These principles may be more important now than they were then. We're vastly more crowded together with more need for observing something like the rules of liberty.

This assessment is based on reading the Constitution for the kinds of powers that are granted to the federal government, and the kinds that are not, rather than literally in either present or historical terms. Both kinds can rationally be adapted to present circumstances, keeping in mind the purposes of the federal government recited in the preamble.

For example, to provide for the common defense, the federal government is granted the power to raise, that is, organize and pay for, an army and a navy. There is no mention of an air force, an electronic code-breaking agency (NSA), or a Central Intelligence Agency. These, though, are all reasonable extensions or evolutions of the functions of an army and navy at the turn of the 19th Century.

Post Roads and Interstates

To promote the general welfare inherent in trade, the federal government was empowered to establish what were then called post-roads.[7] But it wasn't empowered to operate stagecoaches. There's a critical distinction here between providing fixed infrastructure, and the implements that use it. The principles inherent in these distinctions, though, make interstate highways, and air traffic control, legitimate federal functions, but don't cover running buses or airlines. There is nothing in the Constitution, though, to prevent a state or city from doing either, and supporting them with taxes, if that's what their citizens want.

Using the same logic, the federal government could build, or buy, interstate rail lines, and allow multiple companies to operate trains on them, just like trucks on the Interstate. This would not only be legitimate but might even work better than Amtrak.

No National Police

The authority to enact federal laws logically authorizes an FBI to investigate violations, but not a nationwide local police force. That would be a different kind of thing. A national police force to control all crime could easily have been envisioned but wasn't included, so would not be a reasonable extension. The founders knew of the danger to liberty of such a national force, so didn't delegate that power. I doubt many citizens would welcome a national police force in their neighborhood today, independent of local authority.

The implication for liberty is that the federal government was and is intended to possess only powers of the kinds explicitly granted in the Constitution. The federal government, for example, is granted the power to regulate interstate commerce to facilitate a national market. While this is appropriate, we must be on guard to prevent extending this power to cover all commercial activity, or worse yet, to require engaging in any particular commerce.

One tenet of liberty is "I won't lie to or try to trick people." Creating a new federal power by slithering around the absence of a clearly enumerated grant is the same as tricking people but on a very large scale.

Civil Rights

The newly independent States had just come out of a time when they had been dictated to by a distant king and parliament. When it came time to draft a new constitution they knew that forming a central government with power over them was a risky gamble. Some of their leaders, who called themselves *Federalists*, thought that by not granting plenary powers to the new government, leaving these with the States, and by strictly defining the powers the federal government was granted, the rights of the States and the liberty of the people would be safe.

The argument was "If we don't give this new government powers that we don't want it to have, we'll be OK."

Others rather unimaginatively called *Anti-Federalists* suspected this might not be enough and wanted to include a recitation of rights and liberties. The Federalists, though, worried that including a list of liberties could be interpreted as limiting their rights to what was written. Or, they might leave out something that could one day become important. So, they reached a compromise, part of which was to add eight amendments setting out specific rights of the people and the states. These rights would be protected by the Constitution, and the federal government would be given power to enforce them against states.

President Eisenhower exercised this power when he dispatched federal troops to integrate some public schools in Arkansas.

But besides the first eight amendments, in case someone might misinterpret the recitation of rights; the drafters added a ninth to be sure no one would think these were our only rights.

The enumeration in the Constitution, of certain rights, shall not be construed to deny or disparage others retained by the people.[8]

But they still worried that even this might not be enough, so they added a tenth amendment saying they really meant it when they granted only specific, enumerated powers to the federal government.

The powers not delegated to the United States by the Constitution, nor prohibited by it to the States, are reserved to the States respectively, or to the people.

They wanted to be crystal clear that all powers not specifically granted to the new government were retained by the people or the States.

Inherent, not Granted

Together these amendments clarify that our rights regarding government are not granted by the Constitution, certainly not by the government it creates, and that the federal government is to be strictly limited in its scope. The people's natural rights are inalienable and pre-date the Constitution, which only recites a few, possibly for emphasis on rights that had often been abridged by governments.[9]

This is about as clear as anything can be.

For example, freedom of speech is not a First Amendment right. It is a natural right that the Constitution is bound to protect, but it doesn't come from the Constitution.

Similarly, the Second Amendment fundamentally pays homage to the natural right of self-defense but doesn't limit its means to flintlock muzzleloading rifles.

This duality is both a blessing and a curse. The Constitution is clear that we have certain rights, and it's careful not to constrain them, but it does list them. While it might be convenient had the founding fathers defined concepts as crucial as free speech and liberty, it may be better that occasionally we reflect upon them ourselves. The rights protected by the Constitution are not to be parsed by lawyers but understood by citizens and statesmen.

Recent Supreme Court decisions based on the natural right to privacy[10] and the meaning of a well-regulated militia[11] support these concepts as inherent human rights, not just words in a document.[12] They follow directly from the rules of liberty.

This is an ongoing discussion.

Interpreting and Amending

The Constitution is a semi-permanent law of laws embodying our principles of governance. While the states have broad authority subject to specific exceptions, the federal government is not granted power to do whatever is deemed "right" or necessary for the common good. This limitation of federal power is frustrating to those in and out of government who are certain they know what's best for everyone else[13], but that's the price of liberty. Otherwise, federal power would be so broad as to have no limit at all. Liberty would be lost to ambition and transient opinion. States would wither away as distinct independent entities.

While bringing powers granted by the Constitution up to date to reflect modern technology, such as recognizing interstate freeways, railways and even air traffic control as modern versions of post roads, is a legitimate interpretation of the enumerated powers, creating new kinds of powers is not.

Establishing standards for weights and measures and patent protection (constitutionally enumerated powers) can logically be extended to standards for medical drugs and devices, but not to the provision of them to individuals.

If the need for a new kind of federal power seems overwhelming, then we must consider amending the Constitution.

For example, legislators in 1909 recognized that the Constitution did not permit the federal government to tax individual incomes, so they proposed a constitutional amendment to that effect, which had broad support and was soon ratified as the 16th Amendment.[14]

National prohibition of alcoholic beverages was another such instance. The need appeared great, but the Constitution did not grant the power. Sufficient consensus was reached to ratify the Eighteenth Amendment[15] in 1919. After fourteen years of experience with undesired consequences though, the consensus reversed and was recognized by the Twenty-First Amendment. This was as it should be and brings into question the constitutional legitimacy of our present federal prohibition of various other intoxicating drugs.

While drafting and interpreting actual statutes requires the help of lawyers to be precise and specific, constitutional provisions are the people telling the legislators what kinds of laws they will accept. These need to be written and understandable by reasonably well-informed citizens. This should also be the standard by which they are interpreted by courts.

New Powers by Expansive Interpretation

Since the 1930s, federal appellate courts, especially the Supreme Court, have interpreted constitutional grants of federal power expansively, extrapolating them to accommodate legislative and even administrative assertions of entirely new authorities. The implicit assumption is that expansion of federal power is desirable, or even necessary, and undertaking the amendment process would be unduly burdensome.

An unspoken secret is that many legislators, who are charged with the political determination of what is necessary, enable this abdication of power because it lets them avoid deciding hard issues. They'll pass a vague law, leaving critical decisions to administrators, and hope that the Court will either defer to these administrators or make the tough choices for them.[16]

"Well, the Supreme Court has spoken. We'll just have to go along with it."

Over time, a new federal power created this way gains enough beneficiaries to become tacitly accepted, which has the potential to destroy the Court's usefulness as an arbiter of timeless principles. Worse yet, since there is no constitutional provision for this kind of interpretation, the practice has no limit.

The fatuous argument that this is necessary because the Constitution is too hard to amend perfectly illustrates why it is a bulwark of liberty. It is hard to amend precisely because creating new legal principles should be done with great deliberation. Requiring approval by a vast majority of citizens through a slow process prevents hasty alterations to our fundamental principles of governing.

Detours around the Amendment Process

Demagogues, idealists, and committed partisans will always seek detours around the amendment process on the grounds that "My idea is so good it must be implemented without debate or consensus. I shouldn't be required to convince most of the citizens, much less all parts of the county, of the wisdom of my proposal."

The first blatant example of such a detour arose when the Supreme Court invalidated several New Deal laws as exceeding Congress's power. Since Congress has the power to determine the number of justices, President Roosevelt threatened legislation to increase their number, and then to appoint enough supporters to prevail. The nine justices apparently decided they would rather retain some power, rather than none, and approved his progressive policies. Their approvals have subsequently been treated as case law, or precedents, giving them almost the status of constitutional amendments.

Supreme Court Becomes a Super Legislature

Recently, Justices have been nominated by a process that emphasizes ideological reliability, making the Court almost a lifetime super legislature instead of an independent protector of liberty. Five justices of the Supreme Court can create a new constitutional principle by lawyerly interpretation and tortuous extrapolation.[17] No additional vote by anyone is required.

The Court as defined in the Constitution was intended to be insulated from transient passions. It has, though, become politicized to the extent that control of its appointments is a major factor in presidential and senatorial elections. We desperately need sound ideas to improve this situation. I haven't seen any.

The justices obviously don't call their expansive interpretations constitutional amendments, but when they issue a decision that will become a binding precedent for a power not in the text, they're effectively writing one. They often extrapolate from a legitimate power, such as regulation of interstate commerce. For example, in a landmark case, they approved restricting the right of a farmer to grow corn for his chickens because that corn "might otherwise have been sold in interstate commerce." [18]

I call this rhetorical jujitsu. It exploits the ambiguity inherent in any but the most mathematical language to create an interpretation that goes well beyond any rational original meaning or understanding. It is based on searching out what an enumerated power could mean in support of a novel principle, rather than what it clearly means in normal usage, violating the liberty rule according to which I won't try to trick people.

Here's a glaring example that affects everyone.

Social Security

You'll search the Constitution in vain for federal power to create and enforce a system of mandatory old age saving, but this has been popularly accepted even though it contains a strong element of forced income redistribution. Neither feature is founded on any enumerated federal power.

But while it isn't perfect, Social Security has kept a lot of old people out of poverty. It's based on the rationale that our modern economy disconnects workers from traditional sources of community and family support, or perhaps that too many workers are improvident. In either case, it's a plausible response to new conditions and is therefore exactly the kind of federal power that should appear in Section 8 of Article I. It exerts substantial control over practically every citizen, at least as great as setting standards for weights and measures or granting patents. It could easily have been defined and included in an amendment in the 1930s, but it wasn't.[19]

Without getting into the objective merits of the Social Security program, the problem from the viewpoint of liberty is that since it is not based on an enumerated power, it has no limits, which is a direct threat to our civil rights. Anything as large and comprehensive as the Social Security System, no matter how desirable, should be based on clear constitutional authorization. It might not hurt to define its enumerated powers even now, or at least debate them.

The protections of liberty that ought to be provided by a written constitution are being eroded by these stratagems. There's no simple way to correct this. We must think long and hard about how to return to a more constitutional ethos.

Silent Constitution Means No Federal Power

Federal judges should be conservative (small c) regarding expansion of federal power. This doesn't mean they should favor business or wealth or any interest but the plain intent of the Constitution. They also should be able to declare that the Constitution has nothing to say about an issue if trying to make it do that would require tortuous logic beyond a reasonable and prudent extension of the text to modern usage. If the Constitution is silent on an issue, the Congress should not legislate, because it has not the power, and courts should not create new powers from their intuition of what powers it might grant. They should not venture beyond the Constitution to their assessment of current public opinion, even if it's called Social Science,[20] to create new federal powers.

Limited Interpretation

Language, laws, and life being imprecise and changeable, some process for interpreting statutory and constitutional provisions is, however, necessary. Our present arrangement is usually adequate unless the issue requires significant new principles. In such cases, the justices, who are arguably some of our most knowledgeable experts on constitutional principles, are often unable to reach a consensus and the case is decided by a bare majority, like 5 to 4. While this settles the case at hand, it may establish a truly new principle which is an unseemly usurpation of both legislative and popular authority, and the tortuous logic necessary to reach the decision may well leave the principle unclear.

A better way would be to allow the specific case at hand to proceed as now in order to resolve it, but only if decided unanimously or nearly so should the decision be considered precedent in future cases. In closer cases, Congress should consider a possible constitutional amendment expressing a consensus on the issue, which might even be that the issue is not one for federal legislation. If a resulting amendment is approved in the normal way the issue is settled. If it fails, then future court decisions should recognize that. While this process could become somewhat cumbersome, it would avoid the unseemly assault on liberty of five unelected jurists amending the Constitution or creating a law with no public debate.

Only Congress is granted authority, in Article I, Section 1, to enact federal laws. The Supreme Court logically, though not explicitly, has the power to declare a law to be in violation of the Constitution and therefore unenforceable, but it should not have the power to create new ones or otherwise substantially amend them by interpretation. In any event, we need to improve on the present practice.

What might be good criteria for amending the Constitution?

Criteria for Amending the Constitution

The first thing to think about is the rules of liberty. The most relevant ones in this context are those about not tricking people or forcing them to believe what I do. This requires using clear meanings in interpretation and seeking meaningful consensus in amendments.

Humility is helpful here. It means that if I propose an amendment or new interpretation, I'll attempt by argument to convince a large body of citizens of its merits. I won't try to slip it in via novel meanings of words or clever parliamentary maneuver. I'll recognize that approaching a problem from diverse perspectives usually improves on an initial solution.

Simple prudence suggests that a constitutional change, whether it be an interpretation or a formal amendment, that is agreeable to a large majority has a better chance not only of actually working but of surviving the inevitable evolution of power structures and conditions than one barely squeaking by. But, there's never 100% complete agreement on anything, certainly not in a large, diverse nation. So, the objective should be to convince a large majority of the people but realize it won't be everyone.

How large a majority should this be?

The amendment process is neither easy nor quick, but it's possible. The constitutional mechanism that achieves both a large majority and input from diverse states is to require that the legislatures of three-fourths of the states agree to the proposal. This difficulty prevents a bare majority, or even an intensely motivated minority, from gaining tyrannical power. The most recent amendment was adopted in 1992.

Potential State Power

Another prudent approach would be to step back and consider whether states inherently already have the newly desired power. Remember, they have the power to do anything not prohibited by the Constitution. Maybe a new federal power is not really needed. Try selling your idea in your home state and see how it works. If it does, others may emulate it. Or, they may prefer not to. That's the beauty of federalism.

An argument against the state approach is that if the newly suggested government power is enacted by only one or a few states, people who don't like it will move to other states. Think about this for a minute in terms of forcing people to believe what I believe. Do I really want to employ the armed force of government to do this? Maybe the answer tells me something about my proposal.

The federal government was never intended to be pure majority rule. This is one place where our semi-sovereign states are recognized as being real sovereigns with their own identities.

The Constitution was a work of genius when written. But it is not self-enforcing, even by courts. It's up to us. The public must regain control of its basic law of laws

Chapter 6

Full-Service Government with Liberty

Preserving liberty must be the overriding objective of good government,
but it can't be the only objective.

Government enables free people to develop their potential in an environment of liberty. Safety from attack supports this objective directly, but other services support it indirectly. Public policy, the totality of broadly understood policy positions on which legislation and executive action are based, must provide this environment without unduly restricting liberty. Even policy not directly affecting liberty must be crafted with concern for it because government ultimately enforces its policies with physical force — guns and jails. It is not a church where the pastor leads by moral suasion. To be consistent with liberty, any use of force must be circumscribed with great care. Its design is a serious matter.

This chapter examines the major responsibilities undertaken by governments at all levels from the perspective of liberty. Our simple rules are extended to develop principles for assessing important policies and legislation. The guiding principle is to support the development and evolution of humans with their unique gifts and the civil society in which they prosper.

- The **Justice** System is how government directly protects liberty domestically. It clarifies the rules and enforces them on those who choose not to follow them. It's how liberty is preserved between people.

- **National Defense** protects us from foreign powers who would assault our liberty.

- The **Primacy of Civil Society** over government is usually unstated but essential to liberty.

- **Promoting the General Welfare** is a tricky concept to define but crucially important. It justifies much of what government does beyond justice and defense. By itself, it's only an objective and doesn't lead directly to any government powers, but it is supported by many that are large enough to warrant separate consideration.

- **Conserving a healthy environment** is an important aspect of the general welfare forced upon us by the growth of population and our economy.

- **Universal Public Education** is necessary when the public is entrusted with the responsibility for self-government.

- **Immigration** control is a direct expression of sovereignty. Its goal must be to admit people having a respect for liberty and a demonstrated ability and desire to join and contribute to our civic culture.

- **Managing Public Lands** is another expression of sovereignty that supports general welfare over the long term.

- **Assisting Needy persons** is an optional function of government, but a very large one most of us wish it to pursue to some extent.

- **Managing the Economy** is a questionable function that has become a major role of the federal government.

- **Taxes** are necessary to pay for government but have come to play a much larger policy role.

- And finally, **Government Operation,** to respect the rules of liberty, should be non-coercive to individuals, not disrupt civil society, and be as open, honest, and efficient as possible.

This is a long list, but it's what government does, so it all must be considered if we are to employ liberty as a guide to policy. Starting with justice, we will look at each function to see how it relates to liberty, and sometimes suggest alternative approaches more consistent with liberty.

Justice

Liberty is not a natural state of the human condition. Absent a profound change in human nature, there will always be those disposed to violate its rules. The justice system is how we enforce them with actual laws much more detailed than those used here to illustrate principles.

Beyond simply enforcing laws, the essence of justice is its equal and impartial application. In a just society, no one can be allowed to employ the law to gain an advantage over another by virtue of who he or she may be or his or her official position.

Local Control

Because justice necessarily applies State force, it has the potential to itself violate the liberty of both accused and uninvolved individuals. We must be very careful that the laws themselves don't violate liberty. One way we exercise this care is by keeping control of the police power as close as possible to those being policed. Everyone involved, from legislator to suspect to judge, is then more likely to be similarly situated.

In a very real sense, this follows from the self-control rule by which I won't try to force others to believe as I do. An example might be problems such as excessive incarceration for drug offenses when that power is assumed by the federal government at the expense of state sovereignty.

Federal Supremacy

In a contrary situation though, it may be appropriate for the federal government to step in to restrain states from violating basic civil rights. An example would be federal US Attorneys bringing corruption charges against local officials. A former governor of Illinois is in the federal slammer because he tried to sell the Senate seat Barack Obama vacated when he won the presidency.[1] Earlier, President Eisenhower used that supremacy to enforce school integration.

Civil Disputes

Besides enforcing criminal laws, government courts can peacefully adjudicate disputes arising from private contracts or other non-criminal acts, with decisions having the force of law on the dispute at issue. Provision of impartial civil courts applying a stable body of law is essential to a productive economy, distinguishing modern free nations from poorly governed ones. Over time a stable justice system develops a detailed set of precedents and codified laws based on extending the principles of liberty to such subfields as contracts, torts, and crimes.

To retain clear meaning in public discourse, the concept of justice must be limited to these subjects and not expanded to include general fairness or equality in life. While these may be worthy goals, they are so different from administration of just laws that they warrant their own names and analysis.

Criteria for Laws Respecting Liberty

In a constitutional system based on liberty, laws must be

- Clear to those subject to them

- Focused on a single issue
- Clear in policy and the intended scope of executive and judicial discretion
- Based on a strong consensus, not just a bare majority
- Fairly stable, changing only in response to widespread changes in conditions
- Restricted to the minimum force necessary to achieve a constitutional purpose
- Equitable in their provisions, enforcement, and impact
- Applied equally to all, notably including government officials
- Enacted explicitly by the legislature rather than by executive or judicial action
- Impartial as to individuals while allowing for judicial discretion in considering circumstances.

Judicial Discretion

Judicial discretion is essential for fitting provisions of law to specific cases. In rare circumstances, a new expression of a general principle may be drawn from a series of properly decided cases, but this should not be used to extend law beyond that enacted by the legislature. Judicial discretion should be used only as a rational guide to enforcing existing law.

Respect for Diversity

Respect for law is weakened when the power of the State is used by a faction to impose its preferences on the large body of citizens, especially when the issue is one of personal life management. The force of law should be invoked only when essential for enforcing broadly accepted principles of public policy. Civil society must be allowed to evolve organically and to tolerate diversity of opinion as expressed by "I don't try to force others to believe as I do."

Treating Offenders

The final step in enforcement of justice, namely imprisonment, must recognize that losing freedom because of transgression should not be a total loss of liberty. Those in charge of prisons should vigorously enforce the same rules of liberty postulated here and teach them by example.

Defense

A substantial defense establishment protects us from foreign threats ranging from loosely organized religious fanatics to traditional nations with hostile intent. This necessarily requires superior force and is, therefore, a potential threat to liberty, as is the great expense needed to maintain it. These threats are minimized by maintaining civilian control of the military.

Civilian Control

Defense for the nation as a whole is formalized by Article II, Section 2 of the Constitution which grants the president the power of "Commander in Chief of the Army and Navy of the United States." [2]   For individuals, the Second Amendment recognizes the right "To keep and bear arms." [3]

The power of the president as Commander in Chief of our military forces is limited by requiring acts of Congress to raise and support the army and navy and to declare war.[4]   The question of when an armed conflict rises to the status of war, though, remains somewhat unresolved.

The independence of these armed forces is limited by requiring that, besides the president, the highest officer of each branch be a civilian, and that Congress approve and appropriate all their expenses and the appointment of senior officers. There is no self-selected general staff. The army has never been regarded as an independent entity.

As an aside, we can note a serious misinterpretation has crept into public understanding of this presidential power. The president is commander in chief of the armed forces, not of the nation as a whole, in which incorrect manner he (or she) is often mentioned in public by prominent people who should know better.

Civilian control of the military is exemplified by President Truman's relieving General McArthur of his command in a disagreement over strategy during the Korean War. This five-star general, of towering ego and immense prestige and power—he had commanded our forces in the Pacific in defeating Japan, and at the time was almost its emperor—faded away graciously. That's civilian control.

Emergency Action

As with all the great powers of the United States government, the defense power is assumed to be used with prudence and restraint. These are qualities that by their nature cannot be codified or even well quantified. For example, the nature of the threat from intercontinental ballistic missiles armed with nuclear weapons seriously stresses the concept of declaration of war and even civilian control of our forces.

I would certainly not wait for an approaching knife-wielding attacker to make the first cut in my flesh before taking suitable defensive action, such as firing my pistol if I had the foresight to provide myself with one. We would not want the president to wait for an incoming missile to detonate and kill a million citizens before authorizing a defensive or retaliatory attack depending on the circumstances and our capability.

The issue becomes murkier when the threat is only a potential one based on imperfect knowledge, but the likely consequences may be just as disastrous and our ability to counter an actual attack may be uncertain at later points in its evolution. We simply must choose political leaders and military officers with good judgment and the ability to acquire sound advisers. There is no neat recipe for this, but it doesn't seem that our armed forces are much of a threat to liberty.

There are, though, other defense strategies that have the potential to degrade liberty while intending to defend it.

Forward Deployment

Our strategy for almost a century has been to deploy our first line of defense at forward locations well away from our own shores. One rationale for this is to check aggressors where they start, rather than wait for an actual invasion here at home. This, of course, means maintaining significant forces overseas. This is expensive and trying to predict hostile intent is difficult and uncertain.

Another reason for this strategy is that our economy depends on open and free worldwide commerce which in turn relies on shipping and travel free of hostile restrictions anywhere in the world. Examples would include the South China Sea, and the Straits of Malacca and Hormuz.

A third reason for the policy of forward defense is that we feel a somewhat altruistic obligation to defend democratic cultures where they're struggling.

These objectives embroil us in what is somewhat picturesquely called foreign entanglements. President Washington warned against this, but since the Second World War, we've been in it up to our ears. We form alliances with countries that share at least some of our principles, but this sometimes degenerates into supporting governments with which we share little but a common enemy.

So, does the forward defense strategy support or degrade liberty?

The dilemma is moderated somewhat by what's called a "core and gap" strategy[5, 6] suggesting that extending liberty, or at least democracy, has the best chance of success when it spreads gradually from where it already exists to nearby rather than distant lands. The idea is to avoid trying to leapfrog our ideals to isolated illiberal places, like Afghanistan in southwest Asia. Oh well, no policy ever fits a messy world perfectly.

These principles did though lead to NATO and our Pacific alliances. Compared to alternatives, they seem to have worked.

Internal Security

Then there's internal security, especially against terrorist attacks. Their danger to liberty is immediate and personal. The danger is both in the threat itself —there really are hard-to-detect individuals who want to kill us —and in the measures we take to prevent them from doing this.

Waiting for a terrorist to act and then treating the killings as a crime is inadequate because the resulting terror is the objective. These killers are willing to die, so normal law enforcement and punishment are ineffective.

Defending against this kind of threat requires peering into dark, private corners that our traditions of liberty don't want the government to do. We must discover people's motivations and associations before an overt act is committed. Since we don't know who the terrorists are to begin with, we have to look at thousands of innocents to discover the lone zealot planning an attack. Our defense agencies need access to normally private information such as communication records and content to perform this duty.

Privacy

Privacy is a major concern. No one should be prying into the private affairs of citizens or legal residents. Compounding the dilemma, efforts to detect covert terrorists prior to their killing sprees are most effective if the methods of surveillance are not known to the public ultimately responsible for them. They are necessarily secret. This is a perfect formula for an intrusive state.

Authorization in the Constitution for this kind of policing is not clear, but we certainly need to do something of this nature. The principles of liberty we're examining may offer clues to how this might be done.

We certainly have the right to defend ourselves. Our agents in this are people at all levels of government. While we go to great lengths to assure that our secret agents are good people, we can't expect perfection in their integrity or even in their degree of over-enthusiasm for the chase.

Process

Congress must set rules, and someone must verify that they are followed.

We try to achieve this by debating the general scope of surveillance and protection publicly while developing and conducting procedures in great secrecy. Congressional committees and staff presumably selected for prudence and integrity[7] are responsible for oversight, but they operate at too high a level of program abstraction to be effective and have become too politically partisan to be objective. Agencies have inspectors general, similar to police internal affairs bureaus, but they seem to act after problems become public.

We might want to consider forming a corps of equally vetted people outside the chain of direct responsibility for results who are able to monitor operations, make an objective assessment of the balance of security and liberty in practice, and report discrepancies directly to Congress.

We will never fully and finally resolve the conflict between liberty and its protectors. The best we can do is to understand and manage it.

Making the elected president the commander in chief of a professional military and making Congress responsible for funding that military and affirming the appointment of its senior officers seems to be the best of any known system of protecting liberty while providing defense.

Civil Society

Civil society is the web of arrangements among people that facilitate and enrich their lives. It includes businesses, professional associations, corporations and simple transactions at a food truck. It includes churches, fraternal societies, and special interest clubs for everything from automobile enthusiasts to gardeners. It is charities and chambers of commerce. It is friends getting together for dinner or a ball game. It's everything we do in voluntary groups large and small that fill the space between family and government.

Billions of transactions from greetings in the street to corporate mergers reflect and transmit subtle confirmation of existing norms and the incremental changes that spread and grow until they are eventually recognized as new norms. Such changes are properly recognized after the fact and not decreed by authority.

An active civil society keeps liberty alive. Its principles are taught by example in the home and in public. Its enemy is the belief that people should be directed by elites in the name of the "common good," which is a vague term often slipped in surreptitiously to replace general welfare but with a significantly different meaning.

Civil society as such is not featured in the Constitution because the government it defines was clearly meant to be created by and separate from civil society, not to define or manage it. The Founders believed that a society living by Judeo/Christian morality would thrive under such a constitution.[8]

Government is distinguished from civil society by its uniformity and use of coercion. It must treat every citizen equally but with the potential of force so all follow the same rules. This is the equal-treatment aspect of justice. (The fact that we don't always attain this ideal doesn't alter the principle.)

Civil society, though, is by nature heterogeneous and voluntary. One of the best things about it is that it is constantly experimenting with new ways of doing and being with no central control. Government operating this way would be disastrous for liberty. Government is good at setting limits. Civil society dreams and aspires.

Only when a principle of unacceptable behavior is nearly universally held, should a law recognizing that be considered, and then only if clearly necessary. There need not be a law for everything.

Government Not a Church

As federal power has grown, it has become easy to believe that government is actually the structure of society. This is a terrible error because it reduces people to interchangeable elements that can be manipulated to a common design and purpose. Government is not an end in itself but only a tool to help maintain and protect civil society. It should not define, create, control or manage that society.

We should not treat government like a church, expecting adherence to a comprehensive catechism of beliefs. Confusing government with religion turns political disagreement into religious war. History teaches us how that turns out.

Electing the United States president by a broad national franchise tempts some citizens and presidents to endow the person holding that office with leadership authority beyond what is defined in Article II of the Constitution. This temptation should be resisted. The president is not chosen to be the moral leader of a huge national church. He, or she, is elected to enforce federal law, administer a gigantic civil government, command a world-spanning military, and conduct complex and dangerous relations with foreign powers. That's plenty. Seek moral leadership in religion or other parts of civil society.

Federalism is a constitutional expression of civil society in the way it relates states to the federal government. It allows states to have different cultures while retaining the benefits of a national market and a strong federal government in matters of national scope and character. As with any plan for distributing power, it works best when prudently applied. Some recent examples where California is attempting to coerce other states to adopt its mores suggest where limits may lie.[9]

Civil society is not uniform in space or time. What is normal in West Texas may be outré in Boston. This is why much legislation should be left to states rather than the federal government.

While our government has been a bulwark of liberty, it is not as important as our civil society in being a shining example of human potential. Our civil society, not our government, is a prime destination for people around the world seeking a better, freer life.

To summarize: Preserving the health of civil society is a higher priority than expanding government control. Promoting civil society as distinct from government has become increasingly necessary. This includes recognizing when government action is appropriate to solve a supposed problem, and when it isn't. Government is not "what we all do together," nor is it a church. It's a distinct civil entity with lethal enforcement power created to protect liberty and perform certain services.

Liberty does not claim to result in a perfect society. It just enables civil society to create the best one available.

General Welfare

We the People of the United States, in Order to form a more perfect Union, establish Justice, insure domestic Tranquility, provide for the common defense, promote the general Welfare, and secure the Blessings of Liberty to ourselves and our Posterity, do ordain and establish this Constitution for the United States of America.

One purpose of the federal government is to promote the general welfare, but what does that mean?

As with some of the other concepts in the Constitution, and some not even mentioned, we must presume that the idea of the general welfare was so well understood at the time of its writing that the founders felt no need to be more specific. But because it has become so distorted in recent years *we* need to examine it more closely.

General Welfare is an environment or condition and not a function or service. It refers to an environment in which public goods support individual and cooperative efforts at maintaining or improving the conditions of life. In this context, a *good* is any desirable product, environment, or service, not limited to tangible items one might buy in a store.

Public Goods

Public goods are those freely available and not consumed while being enjoyed. They form part of our public environment.

Examples of public goods that support the general welfare include

- Clean air, safe waters, and a generally healthy biosphere
- Public safety, including national defense
- Readily available knowledge
- Public health, such as epidemic control and food safety
- Roads
- Parks
- A system of stable currency
- A well-functioning judicial system

Public goods are available without charge, though they are not without cost to provide. In economic terms, they are "non-exclusive." Furthermore, they are not provided in discrete units such that consumption by one person would make the good unavailable to another. (They are "non-rivalrous.") For example, a good police force makes the streets just as safe for a new arrival as for prior residents. The same would be true for clean air. The costs of providing them are spread more-or-less evenly over all beneficiaries and can't be attributed to any particular consumer.

To further clarify the concept of public goods, consider non-public goods such as a meal, a house, a surgery or a dollar. Consumption of any of these makes that unit unavailable to anyone else. The nature of their consumption makes them non-public.

Not all public goods are provided by government. Many are provided by civil society. An entertaining or educational television program is free for as many people as may wish to consume it. Information on Wikipedia is freely available to all, though many donate to the service. Most libraries are free or nearly so and experience only soft limits to their capacity, so are therefore public goods no matter how they are supported.

Not "The Common Good"

General welfare does not refer to the specific condition, or welfare, of an individual and is not what is loosely called "the Public, or Common, Good." (It's unfortunate that "good" has two distinct meanings in a context where they can be confused. We just need to be careful in using it.)

The loosely defined "common good" includes concepts such as standard of living, personal income, or individual health, each with its own meaning. Using these terms when warranted is crucial for communicating ideas for public policy. If the federal government were to provide them, we would need to add language such as "Provide sufficient food to the people" to the objectives of the Constitution and grant specific powers to realize that purpose.

Federal Provision of Public Goods

Promoting the general welfare means providing public goods, but which ones are the responsibility of the federal government? Clearly, it's not all of them. The federal government was never intended or granted power to provide local police, roads, schools or land-use zoning rules, though these are all legitimate elements of the general welfare. There is no grant, except within the District of Columbia and some federally owned property, of power to make general laws under the police power.[10, 11] The federal government is, though, granted power to provide such public goods as long-distance roads (in colonial times called post roads) with the evident purpose of facilitating commerce. Standardized weights and measures, a common currency, and patent protection are other examples where provision of public goods is assigned to the federal government.

Constitutional objectives and grants of power are clearly different things. It is also clear there is no suggestion in the Constitution that the federal government provide any non-public goods at all.

State Provision of Public Goods

Though the federal government is not granted power to provide any non-public goods, and only some public goods, the states have much more latitude because of their residual sovereignty. They can also exploit this latitude differently, as directed by their voters. But what if some states don't live up to "our" standards of public service?

The claim that the federal government must satisfy some needs because states won't do enough flies directly in the face of the liberty rule that I won't force others to believe as I do. Another way of expressing this is the citizens of Oregon shouldn't use federal power to force the citizens of Nebraska to do as we would in our state.

Federal Provision of Non-Public Goods

A Stolen Concept

Over the past century, advocates for federal spending on a variety of non-public goods have insinuated the practice under the tent of general welfare. They have, in the words of Ayn Rand in her novel Atlas *Shrugged,*[12] stolen the concepts of public goods and general welfare to apply their wide acceptance to the distinctly different concept of personal support.

It should be a crime against discourse to shoehorn an extraneous concept into an already well-accepted one to sell a completely different idea. While language does evolve, purposefully or carelessly altering the usage of a word to include incompatible meanings is a form of fraud. This conceptual error contributes to the ills bedeviling our republic. As we proceed, we will see how it can turn a republic of free citizens into a mob of clients.

Beyond semantics, the illogic of this corrupted interpretation becomes clear when the consequences are considered. The argument is often made by tax-and-spend proponents that Section 8 of Article I authorizes Congress to tax and spend as much as it wants for any purpose by invoking its general welfare clause. This interpretation would obviate the necessity for all the actual enumerations of federal power. There would be no limit on congressional taxing, spending, or authority.

The objective of promoting the general welfare is not a blank check.

A similar argument can be based on the principles of liberty without parsing the Constitution. I deny myself the right to take the property of another for my own use or to give to someone else. That alone is sufficient to deny the legitimacy of the government doing it in my name.

Threat to Legitimate Public Goods

Costs associated with providing personal individual support are overwhelming the federal government's ability to provide public goods that actually promote the general welfare. A small instance of this starvation is seen in recent calls to privatize agencies such as the National Weather Service,[13] which is a perfect example of a public good. The information it produces is available to all without charge, and its product is not diminished by each user. It and others like it, such as air traffic control, are likely to be lost to the increasing cost of providing non-public goods.

A Test for Legitimate Federal Powers

Promoting the general welfare is the rationale for granting the federal government many of the powers enumerated in the Constitution. This means that any new powers placed in the Constitution, and the laws that depend on them, should pass the test of "does this promote the general welfare?"

The federal government presently provides many non-public goods for which its authority is arguable at best. The Constitution demands that only enumerated powers be used for any purpose. This restriction has been increasingly violated for some time and correcting it will take time, wisdom and effort.

Environment

Here's an example of a crying need for a constitutional amendment.

There may be uncertainty about the nature and degree of the threat, but there is good evidence that the natural environment in the United States is at significant risk of being degraded by various forms of pollution. This is a textbook example of a threat to our general welfare.

One liberty rule is I won't dump my garbage on my neighbor's lawn. It recognizes that as a form of attack and an infringement of liberty.

The states clearly have the police power to abate nuisances, and injured people have a right to pursue tort claims for specific damage done by specific polluters, but neither has proven to be a practical or even possible remedy for widespread pollution.

No Federal Authority

The authors of our constitution would have had a hard time foreseeing the growth of our population and industry over the past two centuries. We've only become aware of the negative impact these can have, especially at a national scale, in the last couple of generations.

So, no power to manage or control the environment, or people as they might affect it, is granted to the federal government. No such power is enumerated.

Remember, the constitutional purpose of promoting the general welfare does not, in itself, grant any specific power. But the need for some kind of federal environmental protection, to support the general welfare, including working with other countries, is pretty clear.

What should we do?

Abuse of Authority

What we have done is Congress has passed laws—without reference to constitutionally granted power—and several administrations have adopted regulations loosely based on these laws. The result has been an egregious abuse of authority as when a farmer in northern California faced a $2,800,000 fine for plowing his field.[14]

President Obama entered into an important international agreement, essentially a treaty, without the advice and consent of the Senate.[15] Setting aside the merits of the agreement, this has caused confusion about United States policy on global warming. We've wasted time and political energy on an agreement made without constitutional legitimacy, whether on grounds of enumerated powers or procedure.

There's a well-established, predefined constitutional way to deal with this.

Constitutional Response

States should accept their responsibility under the police power to abate environmental nuisances in their jurisdiction. There is nothing to prevent them from cooperating with each other or using federally developed information. Some will take different approaches depending on their circumstances and public philosophies. Some results will be better than others. All will learn. Among other things, they will discover that some problems are beyond their scope. Actually, they probably know this now.

We must hold a serious national discussion about the nature of the environmental threat to the general welfare. This should be at a fairly high level of abstraction so we can tease out principles applying to the nation as a whole. We need to understand and sufficiently agree on what kinds of things are affected, such as air, water, food, etc.? What kinds of effects are important? What are our goals, not specific solutions? We must agree on the kinds of federal powers appropriate to reaching these goals without unnecessarily infringing on the sovereignty of states or the liberty of their citizens.

Because the federal government, with the tacit acquiescence of the public, has already arrogated to itself power that exceeds constitutional limits, correcting this situation will be difficult and protracted, but it must be done to avoid unchecked federal power.

Until control of interstate pollution can be put on a sound constitutional footing, federal environmental policy should be to enact only regulations clearly necessary to control pollution or damage to the national biosphere that causes more harm than the costs of control. This approach might be possible through a presidential executive order.

Education

The success and perpetuation of our system of government rely not on checks and balances, the Bill of Rights, or a strong military; but on the patriotism, good sense, compromise, decency, and love of order of the people and their unforced fidelity to the constitutional character that pervades our national existence.[16]

We govern ourselves, both in the sense of living by the rules of liberty and being responsible for directing a government that, among other things, codifies and enforces them. We have to direct the government because if we don't, it will direct itself. That doesn't mean we all must know how to manage a national park, command a nuclear submarine, or be a judge. But we have to know the principles that should guide these people, and how to tell if they're being observed.

History shows that it's easy for a people to accept and even be part of an authoritarian form of government. They forget, if they ever knew, the principles and value of liberty. They just trust the leaders. We must do better if we're to preserve liberty. But since liberty doesn't come naturally, it must be taught. And that's the schools. Public schools or even schools in general may not be the only place liberty and government can be taught, but they seem to be the most efficient way for everyone to learn and practice our form of citizenship.

The ready availability of an education in culture and the practical arts (language, math, science, technology etc.) has also been a public good contributing to the general welfare.

The founders understood this but put nothing in the Constitution about how it was to be achieved; perhaps assuming that a normal desire for education, and state initiative, would work this out as it had in the past. There is no enumerated power granted to any of the three federal branches to provide, fund, or regulate education. The states, though, possess this power as an inherent element of their sovereignty.

There is nothing necessarily national about education, and since the Constitution does not grant the federal government any power in this area, its involvement through the federal Department of Education should be terminated. This includes funding. The power to tax extends only to paying for the exercise of enumerated powers.

There is no good reason to place responsibility for education at any level of government higher than the states or local communities.[*] Any argument to the contrary is nothing more than income redistribution and social control on a national scale. Alternative approaches should be encouraged at state discretion, with public schools being only one option among many.

The principle that I won't try to force others to believe as I do, even if I'm convinced they are mistaken, extends to relations between the states and federal government.

Immigration

Immigration created and shaped American history. Many early settlers and later waves of immigrants came to the New World to escape persecution, famine, poverty, unjust laws, or simply to live in the freedom we were developing. In its early decades, the United States had no immigration policy.[17] People who wanted to be part of the new culture of liberty just came and became citizens. Providing succor to the huddled masses,[18] as suggested in the inscription at the base of the Statue of Liberty, while not a formal policy, fit perfectly with the need to populate and control a continent.

---

[*] Racially unequal expenditure of public funds, even by states, is prohibited by federal civil rights law. This is a restriction, not a mandate for management or funding.

Immigration policies around the world run the gamut from encouragement to denial.[19] All countries that allow immigration subject it to quotas of one kind or another.[20] Some are bizarre.[21]

Our policies on immigration, citizenship, and population made sense while our people and nation were growing to occupy what was to them an open land. They now, though, warrant re-examination from the perspectives of liberty and our national interest, given population growth here and abroad, and recent experience with immigrant assimilation.

But before assessing these policies, we must know what they are.

Our Present Policies

Population

Population policy underlies immigration policy. While we have few if any formal policies on population as such, many suggest a preference for more people.

Most nations, including ours, seek economic growth. This usually favors increasing population because a common measure of a nation's economic strength is its Gross Domestic Product (GDP), effectively the sum total of everything done for money in that country. And all things being equal, the more people working, the more goods and services are created.

Another factor is that the hospitality, construction, and food production industries depend on an adequate supply of low-cost workers to fill jobs that the American welfare system has made unattractive for citizens.

With growing life expectancy, an expanding older population requires more workers to support retirement programs based on pay-as-you-go intergenerational income transfer[22] — further motivating policies favoring increasing population.

Evidence of such policy is that we subsidize it. Children bring tax deductions and credits. Most prepaid health plans distinguish only between single policyholders and families without considering their size, even though larger families must cost more to service. Social Security payments to surviving parents assist with child-rearing costs also without regard to the number of children. Welfare programs enable single women to live independently if they have children. At least in California, cities and counties are required by law to plan for their "fair share"[23] of a region's expected increase in population. While not explicitly declaring a policy of "more people," these regulations and practices tacitly acknowledge and enable one. None encourage a stable population.

Immigration Policy

Melting Pot

American public culture is built upon rights developed over centuries, primarily in Great Britain.[24] Most western nations have adopted similar principles, but many places that supply immigrants have not.[*] We cherish our "melting pot" tradition by which immigrants become proud Americans, but that is eroding. Our immigration policy lately has tended away from assimilating immigrants into American culture and toward multiculturalism, identity politics, and unification of extended families.

Complexity

Our immigration laws are complex. It takes 13,000 attorneys of the American Immigration Lawyers Association to navigate them.[25] We admit as permanent legal residents about a million people a year.[26] It's inherently hard to say, but there evidently are also roughly three or four hundred thousand illegal immigrants annually.[27] Immigration is a factor in elections at all levels of government.[28] Immigration to the United States is a valuable commodity with many willing to pay thousands of dollars to enter legally or illegally.[29]

---

[*] How many of the world's people can actually practice our level of freedom of speech, religion, women's equality or security of property?

Formal Policy in Laws

Immigration policy has two distinct parts, a formal legal one and an ad-hoc semi-legal popular one. The formal policy for admitting permanent residents[30] emphasizes family unification as a more-or-less open-ended entitlement, while refugees and some skilled workers and entrepreneurs are subject to quotas.[31]

Ad-Hoc Informal Policy

The ad-hoc semi-legal part of our policy is based on ignoring or flouting federal immigration law. Its first principle is that anyone who physically enters the United States, whether by surreptitious border crossing or overstaying a valid visa, should be allowed to remain here without negative consequence. Employment and public benefits should be accessible without hindrance or discrimination. Undocumented aliens, especially unaccompanied minors, who show up at a border post and say "asylum" should not be denied entry but taken in for "processing", which usually leads to their being allowed to remain for years while their case is adjudicated.[32, 33] Many paroled this way simply never appear for further adjudication, and they are seldom actively pursued.[34]

The rationale for the ad-hoc policy is that fairness and a sense of cultural equivalence demand that the United States make its advantages available to all without restriction. Many cities and some states, such as Oregon,[35] have adopted formal laws and practices to provide "sanctuary"[36] to illegal aliens,[37] whom they term "undocumented migrants" or some other euphemism.

Citizenship

Our policy on citizenship itself is straightforward. Anyone born in the US, or of a US citizen anywhere,[38] is a citizen. This "birthright" citizenship[39] is rare worldwide.[40] While there is disagreement about its exact meaning and provenance, it is based on the 14th Amendment to the Constitution.

A legal permanent resident for five years can become a citizen by passing (at a 60% level) an oral quiz[41] consisting of an eclectic mix ranging from significant principles to historical trivia. There are no numerical or quota limitations on applying for citizenship beyond being a legal permanent resident.

Assessing our Policies

Our heritage values compassion and generosity. It tells us to feed the hungry and comfort the afflicted. It leads us to take in victims of cruel regimes as refugees. Granting asylum though is not without cost. It feels good to be generous and compassionate but we must look beyond worthy beneficiaries to potential negative consequences to liberty. There is also some risk in granting permanent residency to people who see only the material wealth or superficial personal freedom visible from afar and who neither understand nor value the principles of liberty that support them.

Regulating immigration to serve our national interest shouldn't need justifying, but in the past few years, prominent American politicians have advocated a borderless world where vague international norms take precedence over the United States Constitution. [42, 43]

Conflicting Cultures

Restricting immigration is neither selfish nor chauvinistic. We value certain standards of public life. Admitting people with strongly held incompatible standards would require us or them to change. If there is any validity in the belief that our libertarian culture is superior to some others, admitting such immigrants in numbers sufficient to dilute that culture would make no sense. Believing that such immigrants would alter their beliefs to assimilate into our culture seems hubristic or at least wishful thinking.

A rule-based immigration bureaucracy having limited resources will find such evaluation difficult because we recoil from ideological or religious tests. We don't like to inquire into people's beliefs. But because the United States of America is based on an ideology and not on heredity or geography, we must do it.

Permanent Population Growth

Seeking to support our aging population by continually importing low-cost workers is a recipe for uncontrolled population growth because these workers and their offspring eventually become an even larger cohort of old people, perpetuating the increase. This is more than reminiscent of a Ponzi scheme in which an increasing number of new suckers are needed to make promised payments to earlier marks. Liberty, economic viability, and the environment are casualties.

Pressure to import low-cost workers is an instance of flawed policy creating problems we try to ameliorate by pursuing additional flawed policies rather than correcting the original error. We must recognize that simply increasing our population no longer contributes to our general welfare. Our goal should be greater per-capita GDP rather than just a larger total.

Curtailing our dependence on an increasing population is compatible with liberty. We should do whatever is necessary to facilitate working age citizens saving adequately for their old age, including likely increases in their medical costs. This might include

- Taxing spending rather than earning or saving
- Eliminating legislators from decisions about saving — this means privatizing Social Security to the greatest extent possible
- Eliminating welfare and disability policies that discourage low-skill employment.

These reforms will reduce central control and dependence on government with their attendant assaults on liberty. Immigration policy then can be developed free from the burden of coping with the effects of bad domestic policy.

Beyond immigration or population policy, our emphasis should shift from new development using new land and resources to improving the quality of what we have. We must all learn to contribute and compete in a complex and sustainable economy. Simply showing up and doing as told is no longer enough. Anyone who wants to live well these days must be a learner and adapter throughout life. This is a lesson from evolution.

Reduced Productivity and Assimilation

Our present policy degrades rather than improves the productivity of our workforce and the appreciation of liberty by our citizens. We emphasize what is called chain immigration by which relatives to the nth degree are admitted regardless of their likelihood of improving our standard of living or culture of liberty. Many are poor uneducated people ill-equipped to understand our culture or the idea of liberty, not to mention our language.[44] Being unable to participate in the advanced aspects of our economy and culture, and probably uninterested in them, they remain isolated in their own communities subject to manipulation by demagogues.

Having access to American standards of social services, menial work paying vastly more than they could earn at home, and enjoying relative freedom from violence, these chain migrants are grateful to those they regard as having given them these things. If granted the vote, they can be a force for tyranny. This is a patently poor immigration policy.

Rejection of Valuable Immigrants

In contrast to chain immigration, we apparently send home foreign graduates of our universities who should be prime candidates for citizenship.

Our policies have become intertwined and corrupted, with multiple agendas hidden behind rampant sanctimony. Reform will be slow and painful, but we must start now to avoid losing our culture of liberty. We must recognize who we are and what is in our national interest.

National Identity

So then, who are we?

One thing we're not defined by is genetics. Our identity myth is that our principles and social practices create one nation out of people from many origins. We are almost uniquely defined by our principles of liberty, which are at least unusual in the world. Presumably, we want to secure and protect this liberty.

We are also, though, defined in part simply by where we are. We are a nation of people who inhabit a particular place. We're not citizens of the world. We are citizens of the United States of America, and it makes a difference.

Citizenship means freely obeying a specific set of laws. We don't want the rest of the world to make our laws, and we shouldn't want to make theirs. We can all think of foreign customs, laws or governing practices under which we would not want to live.

Responsibility to Citizens of Foreign Countries

Where then are the responsibilities? I suggest that our primary responsibility must be to our own nation and people. We should be good neighbors by not harming other nations. We can even assist and cooperate with them. But we should not feel responsible for solving their local problems.

It's a fact there are hundreds of millions of people around the world in dire straits who would be greatly relieved to live under our umbrella of liberty and prosperity. But we simply don't have the resources to make them all happy, certainly not by bringing them here. If the problems immigrants wish to escape are caused by inadequate governance of their country, responsibility for changing that rests with them, not us.

Population here and abroad is approaching some kind of limit. Biology, geography, and physics of the earth's thermal balance tell us this is true even though we don't know exactly how it will manifest. Some parts of the world already experience regular famine. In the US, population pressure appears as water rationing, air pollution, and simple congestion as well as being a factor in global warming. Quality of life suffers as more people are forced to live closer together with more restrictions.

We have neither the physical or ecological space to accommodate all who wish to live here at our accustomed standard of living, nor are we able to bring them all up to our standards of liberty.

Teach Liberty by Example

What can we do for them? One way to help is to develop and exhibit a working model of liberty. We can teach it directly through educational and cultural exchange, and indirectly by example. Sometimes, we may be able to offer direct assistance in bringing their home countries closer to our standards of liberty and in solving their population problems. Experience and data show that when western enlightenment ideas and practices have taken root where they've been missing, more people have been raised from poverty and tyranny than by any other form of assistance. Democracy and women's rights (which reduces population growth) have exploded throughout the world in the past half-century.[45] The point of this observation is that improvement in liberty, or at least democracy, is possible overseas, relieving us of some of this burden.

Military Protection

In extreme cases, where we have the capability, we could consider, very carefully, providing temporary military protection in "safety zones" to people suffering acute tyranny or active genocide while they sort it out themselves. But we must be cautious and prudent in how we do that because many previous efforts have failed miserably.

Improving Immigration Results

Principles

Unless we want to limit immigration by making America unattractive, there will always be more people who want to share in our bounty, both materially and of liberty, than we can accommodate. This is just a reflection of the earth's growing population and its finite carrying capacity. What should be our criteria for immigration?

Select for Potential Contributors

Permanent immigrant status is a valuable privilege to be earned by demonstrated or potential contribution to our standard of living and our environment of liberty.

We must select immigrants for an anticipated ability to assimilate into and contribute to our economy and our culture of liberty.

The only way to improve our per-capita GDP through immigration is to admit people likely to create more wealth than those already here and working. Canada has tried this and it works.[46] Admitting people with demonstrated skills and motivation for advancing technology or economic dynamism has been shown to add employment and raise productivity and standard of living. Educational achievement, including proficiency in English, might be a reasonable proxy for these attributes.

Silicon Valley is full of vibrant new businesses started and staffed by immigrants. We also attract world-class artists of all kinds. Immigration policy needs to select for such people.

It might also be worthwhile, though, to track the long-term history of the families of such immigrants to be sure that the "second-generation" alienation effect is not pronounced,

93

especially as it might manifest in different cultural groups. Again, the object would be to tailor immigration so it improves rather than degrades civil society.

Assure Our Safety

One criterion should be a lack of criminal history. This might be hard to determine in some countries, but we must try.

Accommodating large numbers of legitimate refugees is difficult enough. When asylum seekers are infiltrated by actual or potentially hostile agents, the task takes on an entirely new dimension. We now face the possibility that individuals either formally trained or self-motivated acting as lethal agents of hostile foreign powers will slip into our country in the guise of refugees from civil war. The Boston Bombers[47] entered this way. The possibility of being killed by a terrorist is certainly a threat to liberty.

But before assessing how this threat might affect immigration, the tone of current discourse suggests that we need first to establish that it is even worth considering and that immigration policy should play a role. This is because of arguments that go something like "The number of Americans killed by terrorism is so small compared to those who die in automobile accidents or from preventable disease that there is little point in devoting much attention to it." Or "Treating people from some region or of some religion differently is unfair." Appendix A examines these issues to clarify the security factors relevant to immigration and concludes that we must recognize the nature of this threat and overcome our reluctance to inquire into visa applicants' backgrounds including religion and personal beliefs.

Policies

Immigration policies should:

- Recognize that immigration to the US is not a right but a privilege we may grant based solely on potential benefit to our general welfare

- Emphasize skills and an attachment to liberty over unification of extended families
- Eliminate birthright citizenship for children of non-citizens
- Emphasize assimilation by minimizing accommodation of foreign language in government transactions
- Enact strong controls on hiring non-citizens not having a suitable visa
- Drastically simplify and shorten the process for removing illegal entrants
- Revise our asylum laws to reflect our inability to correct major foreign injustices simply by admitting the victims
- Permit temporary guest workers such as in the old Bracero program,[48] while correcting the problems that have plagued similar programs in Europe
- Do whatever is necessary to assure that immigrants are not security threats.

These thumbnail policies are neither complete nor probably even the best possible, but they introduce some realism and suggest how our present policies can be improved to both stabilize our population and improve our standard of living while protecting liberty.

Public Property

Managing public lands and other property promotes the general welfare. The commons are there to be used, but how and by whom?

The public benefit may be the use itself, as in enjoying a public park or driving on a road. Or it could result from permitted exclusive use by businesses that provide something of value to the public, such as lumber, minerals, livestock, energy or communication.

Use of public property is always subject to conditions, usually that the use not diminish the property unless the use itself is extraction of a resource, and then ancillary damage should be minimized.

Western Lands

For about a century after the nation's founding, full ownership of public land was granted on condition that a homesteader or miner develop a specific piece of property to produce crops or minerals. Railroad developers were offered significant land as an incentive to build rail lines. From the viewpoint of liberty, a major value was supporting the development of a large body of independent citizen settlers able to provide needed goods and services to the rest of the country.

Acquiring title to public property is a thing of the past. In the West, though, huge tracts remain in federal ownership, with some available to private operators for sustainable productive uses such as grazing or resource extraction. This has worked remarkably well as a means for contributing to the general welfare by making such products available.

The past few decades though have seen the process dominated by advocates of an "Earth first" policy in which preserving land in a natural state is the primary priority, leading to underuse of much of it. The inability to sustainably produce lumber from federal forest lands in Southern Oregon is an example.[49] States are also unable to exercise their sovereign right to regulate forest practices to mitigate the fire and smoke hazard coming from federal lands.

In a different kind of use, thousands of square miles of public land in the West are devoted to national parks, which are a shining example of using public land for the general welfare. They are open to all for modest user fees. They provide education about nature and history, world-class opportunities for recreation, inspire respect for our national heritage, and preserve natural spaces for their own value. They absorb a minuscule fraction of the federal budget, giving us a genuine bargain for their cost.

Spectrum

An intangible, but valuable public property managed by the federal government is the radio spectrum, that ethereal space carrying much of the communication that makes modern life possible. This includes everything from life-saving police and fire radios to weather satellites, radio and TV, cell phones and your home's computer router. This finite resource is allocated by the Federal Communications Commission (FCC) according to rules established by Congress. Some of the spectrum is allocated based on officially determined "public interest, convenience, and necessity",[50] while the rest is sold or leased via auction.[51] Strict rules allow millions of us to use this resource without interfering (excessively) with each other.

No Appropriation

Most public property is generally available to all of us, but that doesn't mean we can use it as though we owned it. It should be obvious that being a member of the public doesn't give me a right to occupy or otherwise use public property on my own terms. I must observe the conditions set by the public entity that owns or controls it.

While this limitation should be obvious, occasionally individuals lose sight of it and act as though it doesn't apply to them. Recently, a handful of longtime holders of grazing permits occupied a wildlife refuge in Oregon to protest federal control of large amounts of land in their vicinity, with fatal results.[52]

All levels of government make roads, rivers, parks, and beaches available for public use. Cities generally provide, or mandate, sidewalks through business and some residential areas. Public buildings are generally open to the public for a variety of uses. These uses are just as conditional as use of other common property. I can drive on the roads so long as I obey traffic laws. I can enjoy the beach, but I can't mine the sand or build a pier without special permission. I can walk around town on the sidewalks, or peacefully enter most public buildings, but I can't appropriate space in or on them. I'm not allowed to prevent others from using these common properties. Many cities are currently struggling to control violations of this principle, with varying degrees of success. [53, 54]

The lesson from these examples is that maintaining peace and order has a higher priority than allowing individuals to decide on their own the proper use of public property. The liberty rule about not taking others' or the public's "stuff" is a good one.

Transfer Payments

Present Programs

The federal government spends more than half its budget[55] on direct support to individuals via a multitude of baroque mechanisms. The big ones are Social Security including its disability feature, Medicare, Medicaid, the Affordable Care Act, Unemployment Insurance, Food Stamps, Student Aid, grants to states, public housing, and probably more. (Transfers in this context don't include earned payments such as government purchases, salaries, and retirement benefits.)

The flow is almost impossible to characterize. Many people pay taxes but also receive benefits. Some money comes from artificially high charges such as inflated health insurance premiums imposed on young healthy people to subsidize lower premiums for older sicker people, thus don't appear as taxes. Federal mandates require businesses and local agencies to provide services that end up being paid for by people not using them, like the mystery charges on your telephone bill. A large part comes from borrowing that at least in principle must be repaid by future taxpayers.

Mandatory Appropriations

Congress funds these programs as a class of uncontrollable expenses termed "non-discretionary" or mandatory. The costs are determined by formula and executive rulings and have become, depending on how they're measured, the largest part of the federal budget.

Congress no longer has effective power of the purse. Well, not quite. What it has done is put these programs on autopilot so that while the members could theoretically repeal or amend the automatic appropriations, they have relieved themselves of the responsibility of voting for these ever-increasing expenses.[56] This is a shameful abdication of the power they were elected to wield. The consent of the governed is no longer necessary to expend the largest part of the federal budget.

Votes for Sale

Our national political leaders have discovered they can create voting majorities by promising ever-increasing benefits. Nearly half the US population lives in a household receiving some form of federal financial benefit.[57,58] Many are totally dependent on such aid.[59] Some farm operators depend on federal subsidies or market restrictions.[60] This makes both kinds of recipients dependent on the government, which changes the nature of citizenship and questions the meaning of liberty. Is a person free if he is dependent on others? Does liberty even matter to a person in that situation?

While the money is "free" to recipients, they still must forcefully express their needs to their representatives. Federal government decisions having major consequences for individuals are a direct cause of severe polarization and an unhealthy intensity[61] in our politics.

The Founding Fathers knew the ability to effectively vote ourselves entitlements to other people's property is a potential flaw in democracy. They even warned us about it,[62] yet it has come to pass.

Policy Issues

The basic policy question is how to assist those in need without seriously infringing on liberty, both for payers and receivers. A subsidiary issue is how to apportion responsibility between civil society, the states, and the federal government.

Justifying these programs by claiming that we are all empathetic, so authorize the government to collect the appropriate amount from each of us and distribute it as we would if we could denies the differences inherent in people's motivations, desires, and intentions. A process looming this large in the lives of so many diverse givers and receivers cannot be done well by an impersonal rules-based bureaucracy. Trying to do so ignores or denies the moral agency of humans.

Institutionalizing the human emotion of empathy in government that by its nature cannot be empathetic is an impossible goal. Government cannot feel sympathy, empathy or anything else. It lacks the necessary soul.

At the top of the pyramid, Congress is ill-suited to debate and decide the moral factors necessary to make universal rules for empathy, compassion or charity. What is the correct amount to extract from and provide to every person? What is to be the punishment for a citizen failing to make the right moral choices about charity? Can a choice be moral when coerced?

Misplaced Responsibility

There is no compelling federal interest in providing living expenses for individuals, nor is there any such constitutionally enumerated federal power,[63] so any responsibility for such support falls properly to the states and/or civil society. Relying on the general welfare clauses in the Constitution is not supported by the meaning and structure of that document. The states also must recognize that government funding inevitably means political and bureaucratic control by detailed rules, whereas the nature of the problem calls for individual personal connection and empathy.

To emphasize the lack of federal responsibility for providing income support, realize it is an inherently individual matter of personal need. Nothing is national or interstate about that need any more than the need to prevent burglary or get sufficient exercise. These needs occur everywhere, but not as national events. A national army is necessary for defense, but not for local policing. This is why the Constitution is written the way it is.

History

How did we come to our present unsustainable state?

Prior to the twentieth century, the impulse to assist was expressed locally. In some places and times, it was as charity from the better off to those clearly stressed and dependent, such as Hull House in Chicago.[64] Sometimes it was through voluntary associations of similarly-situated people, usually factory workers, based on reciprocal altruism. These associations were called friendly[65] or fraternal societies and often evolved into mutual (not for profit) insurance companies. Then there were churches, which even today play a small role by hosting free meals prepared and served by members. Common factors in all these arrangements were close physical or social connection between providers and recipients, and their voluntary nature.

In the 1930s massive failure of western agriculture, migration of millions from farming to industry, and a financial collapse led to widespread poverty as chronicled by Dorothea Lange in her heart-wrenching photographs of the iconic Migrant Mother[66] and others. Poor people were stranded in unfamiliar places without the ability to live on the land and isolated from earlier forms of family and community assistance.

The world was becoming infatuated with central planning in the forms of Communism, Fascism, and Fabian Socialism—and doubtful of the American experiment. The response by President Roosevelt in his 1932 New Deal was to create huge federal programs to alleviate poverty (Social Security Administration, The National Recovery Administration, Works Progress Administration and others). These programs mitigated the abject destitution of the 30s, but still many people had well-below-average living conditions, which eventually led to the War on Poverty[67] in 1964.

The migration of public assistance from local institutions to the federal government didn't happen because of some force of nature. It was chosen by our leaders for what seemed at the time to be good reasons. What were they? I don't know the answer to this, or even if there is a single answer, but here are some possibilities.

- That's where the money is, or, in more detail:
- The federal government can print money and run a deficit, while states can't
- The source of federal money is so remote it seems magic
- Some states have more access to tax money than others
- Residents of some states "need" public assistance more than others
- It's harder for taxpayers to exit from the US than from a state
- Taxpayers have less influence on federal than on state laws
- Taking credit for largesse is a sure way to gain votes and power

Collateral Damage

Poverty has not only survived the War on Poverty [68] but collateral damage from friendly fire, to continue the war metaphor, has been severe, with casualties ranging from walking wounded to fatalities. Bureaucratizing compassionate intent has led to programs that enable dependency not on a nearby person who knows and cares about the recipient and may be able to assist him or her to rise into respectable self-sufficiency, but on civil servants applying rigid rules laid down by a distant administrator.

Self-Respect

The deepest metaphorical wounds are to the self-respect of the recipients. They manifest as dissolution of family structures and weakening of community trust and the impulse to reciprocal altruism. Young people are free from the need for personal planning and fail to develop into responsible adults.[69] They know in their hearts that no one needs them. Recipients live from welfare check to welfare check avoiding regular paying work or accumulation of savings to remain eligible for benefits.

When the responsibilities of parenting — not just feeding children but coaching them into adulthood — are given up to a distant government or a street gang of contemporaries, the local world degenerates into an animal culture. "Role Model" may be an overworked term, but when the only visible adults live on welfare checks or crime, the wonder is that any children develop positively, much less gain an understanding of or appreciation for liberty.

It is simply wrong to think that everyone should be able to "follow his bliss". This error isn't as much a matter of government policy as a disease of affluence. It infects dreamers or elites who live on trust funds, have sinecures in academia or government, or have been phenomenally successful in entertainment, technology, or hedge funds. They don't realize most people work because they must support themselves. They also don't appreciate the emotional reward of doing something that other people value enough to pay for it.

Philosophers have known for some time, and academics are now realizing that work is the basis not only for self-worth but for ties that form a healthy community. [70] The recent movement to instill artificial self-esteem creates nothing more than bravado and false expectations because it is not based on earned respect.[71] We are left with adults in despair because slogans and marches cannot create dignity where it does not exist.

Withdrawal from Work

Anything that substantially reduces the connection between work and survival will likely weaken the motivation to work.

It's difficult to get a handle on the reasons for these problems, or even what they are. Our measures of economic and social health are out of date. The unemployment rate ignores people who could work but have given up looking or don't even want to work.[72] This increasing social malaise shows up in the percentage of working age men not even interested in working. Nicholas Eberstadt[73] reports in *Men Without Work* that only about one in seven prime-age men who have left the workforce state that a lack of jobs is the main reason for their departure. He concludes that "One of the critical determinants of being in the workforce in America today is wanting to be in it."

We need not speculate too much about this. As expanding entitlements have allowed more people to depend on others for their basic needs, the participation of adult men in the US labor force (illustrated in the chart below) has decreased from about 86 percent in 1950 to 72 percent in 2015, and is projected to fall to 67 percent (just two out of three) by 2040.[74] This withdrawal from work[75] is much more serious than the unemployment rate that fluctuates with transient economic conditions.

Labor Force Particpation by Adult Men

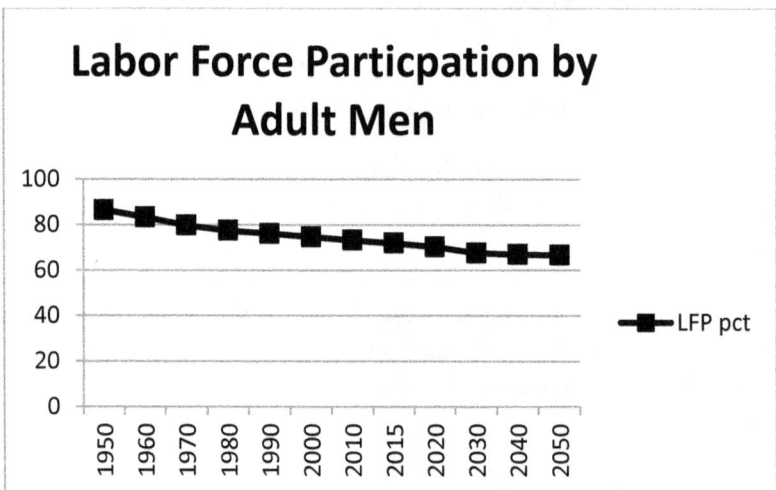

Full-Service Government with Liberty

We must ask what is likely to be the effect on the self-worth, or perceived independence, of men who don't support themselves. Will dependent people be strong believers in or supporters of liberty,[76] one of the main tenets of which is to not take property from others? In a larger context, how much would the productivity of workers need to increase just to maintain our average standard of living when a third of adult men aren't producing anything?

Disability Replaces Welfare

Prior reforms may have reduced welfare rolls,[77] but disability payments have skyrocketed at a time when industrial injuries have plummeted.[78] Some of this increase is visible in excess disbursements from the social security system, but much of it hides in worker's compensation and other forms of early retirement based on adjudicated physical or mental conditions. People go to great lengths to "get on" disability. The costs are dispersed and mostly hidden from view, showing up only as an increase in the cost of living. The result for recipients is an increase in dependence, which after a period of satisfaction at beating the system must lead to the same despair or loss of self-respect described earlier.

Guaranteed Income

Despite clear evidence that long-term dependence on public assistance causes a variety of social ills, the idea doesn't die. Even some of its critics dream that procedural modifications can alleviate the damage. A perennial nostrum is the guaranteed annual income or in its most recent incarnation a Universal Basic Income (UBI).[79] The idea is to replace all present transfer payments with a single monthly payment to everyone, which would be sufficient to live on and be phased out only gradually as an individual increased his own earnings. This was actually tried in Finland. It lasted about a year.[80] While the economic and fiscal impacts might or might not work out, the psychological damage to people not working would be the same as discussed here.[81]

Misleading, Forced Savings

Another form of collateral damage from the war on poverty is that to garner voter acceptance, the largest income transfer programs are promoted as benefitting not only those actually needing help but most of the middle class. The real problem is that Americans don't save enough for their old age. A back-of-the-envelope calculation[82] based on working 40 years over an 80-year life suggests that we need to devote close to half our working income to raising our children and saving for our old age.

To solve this widespread personal problem and to prevent a few people from being destitute in their old age or unable to obtain medical care, the entire population is forcefully enrolled with the promise that their situation will be improved, which seldom works out to be true.[83]

The Social Security program was sold on the false claim that each individual pays into a dedicated savings account of his own. In fact, it's not really savings, and it's certainly not investing. The participants don't actually own anything. It's really a pay-as-you-go scheme to transfer current income from young to old. It creates tenuous entitlements rather than true ownership. Its contributions and entitlements are determined politically so we're forced to compete in that arena for our personal well-being, again making us clients of the government.

Most people don't realize they could do better by planning, saving and insuring on their own. Obviously, we can't all get richer by taking wealth from each other.

One of the great distinctions between humans and other animals, the ability and necessity to make and follow long-term life plans, is blurred by the widespread socialization of that process. When responsibility for caring for the future of oneself and one's family is turned over to an impersonal agency a crucial element of humanity is lost.

Respect for Government

The income-support model has damaged public perception of and respect for the federal government just as it has corroded our culture. As measured by its expenditures, the federal government has become mostly an income transferring, economy managing, debt-incurring, dependence fostering machine. The legitimacy necessary for national defense, regulation of relations between the states and with foreign powers, and promotion of the general welfare is critical to liberty and should not be squandered by using government power for tasks beyond those enumerated and widely accepted as appropriate and necessary. We must not weaken respect for government by requiring it to do that for which it is ill-suited.

Civil Society

Yet another form of collateral damage from the war on poverty has been to civil society organizations and individuals who at one time played a major role in assisting their less fortunate brothers and sisters. It's hard to compete with a bureaucracy that has essentially unlimited resources, access to coercive force and is poorly suited to motivate recipients to examine their lives for ways to improve their situations.

Mortality

The most severe form of collateral damage is an actual increase in mortality. Public statistics show that less-educated white men are dying younger than in the past, in contrast to all other measures of life expectancy.[84] This mortality is associated with increases in self-destructive behavior such as poor-quality diet (not insufficient calories), alcohol, and drugs, which in turn are associated with not seeking employment or otherwise not taking on responsibility.

A Better Policy

Could programs that spend half the federal budget on transfer payments be reformed to provide more effective assistance, impose less collateral damage, restore lost liberty, and cost less?

The principles of liberty teach me not to take the property of another, and by extension, the government I and the other citizens create cannot have this right either. At the same time, most of us wish to assist fellow citizens faced with insurmountable burdens. It's part of the feeling of community that makes a group of people a nation.

There need be no conflict here. Recognizing that the federal government has no legitimate power to take from and give property to individuals does not mean I and other citizens are precluded from making our own gifts. But that might not be enough. How should this impulse be extended beyond voluntary charity to a justifiable program of public goods supporting the general welfare?

Public Goods, Not Entitlements

Any reform must recognize that most citizens can manage their own affairs and should be allowed to do so. But some lack the life skills to make and follow a successful long-term plan in our complex and mobile society. Compassion demands this latter group be assisted in becoming as self-sufficient as possible. This sounds like education, which is a public good promoting the general welfare, but of a special kind.

The overall concept should be liberty, independence, and responsibility for the vast majority of citizens, carefully tailored long-term care and life management for a few truly helpless souls, and a different kind of short-term assistance for those not quite able to manage, or who suffer a temporary hardship. Public assistance should not provide long-term support for the common expenses of most people most of the time. Poverty should be corrected, not made tolerable.

Reform Principles

The objectives for assistance should be:

- Adequate diet and shelter for all
- Reversal of the negative trend in labor force participation, especially of men
- Major reductions in program cost relative to recent history
- Elimination of mandatory appropriations.

The idea here is that no one starves or "dies in the streets" and people living on the fringes of the economy are given appropriate and effective assistance in joining it. The goal is employment.

The main principles would be

- Replace cash or voucher subsidies with direct services for food, shelter, and counseling.
- Replace entitlement qualifications with incentives for recipients to be self-supporting to the extent possible.
- Replace welfare offices and clerks behind windows with small, local, private agencies emphasizing personal contact.
- Provide incentives for service providers to meet program objectives instead of service levels.

This discussion is not limited to programs explicitly described as welfare, but also the much larger programs sold as participatory insurance but which have become complex income transfer schemes. We should eliminate, reduce or significantly amend Social Security, Medicare, Obamacare, housing subsidies, disability and long-term unemployment programs.

The remainder of this section introduces concepts for replacing parts of the current welfare and income transfer programs. Any description in a few pages that alters half the federal budget is necessarily incomplete but may point the way to better results at less cost in money, lives, and liberty.

Personal Savings

Social Security should be replaced with tax reforms that enable and encourage self-supporting citizens to invest similar amounts into personal, wholly-owned savings for their old age. This would shift the model from one of government-mediated intergenerational income transfer to one of lifetime personal savings transitioning to a lifetime annuity at retirement.[85] The gains for individuals would be greater retirement income because of the greater lifetime return from equities than from government bonds, and the security and satisfaction of protecting one's savings from arbitrary legislative decisions. The public gains would be an increase in capital available for productive investment and a vast reduction in federal spending.

By investing in productive assets, a person is making and following his own plan under his own control, and gaining satisfaction from knowing he or she is an independent responsible adult. This is the only way to gain self-respect. Transferring this responsibility to an impersonal "society" or government is a recipe for dependency and its ills. Investments, along with insurance that spreads the risk of unusual losses over a large number of similarly situated people, are the modern equivalent to an extended family. Savings are pooled in productive enterprises such as index funds which grow with accumulated profits that can be enjoyed later in life.

A common argument against the idea of personal savings is that equity investments are subject to market volatility. While this is true for short periods, over a working lifetime there is no better way to accumulate the wealth to support a comfortable old age.[86]

Retaining the coercive nature of the present system can be a matter for debate. Liberty pulls one way and the reality of people's ability and inclination to make and follow long-term plans pulls the other. We are accustomed to paying about 15% of our income into Social Security, so this may be a hint. Transitioning from taxing income to taxing expenditures would also help but is not essential to the idea. The government's role would be to monitor and assure the safety and soundness of the commercial and non-profit investment firms implementing the program and enforce any rules requiring participation.

This is not a new, untried concept in retirement saving. The Teacher's Insurance Annuity Association and College Retirement Equities Fund (TIAA/CREF) is a successful example with which the author is personally familiar.[87] An equitable transition from the present Social Security System would be expensive in the short run because of the current and close retirees who have paid taxes but for whom there are insufficient actual savings to cover their promised benefits. But this shortfall is already imminent, and the new system will pay off in the longer term when the present system would be broke anyway.

Assistance for Independence

Savings reform, though, is for people with an income, which fortunately includes most of us. Its purpose is to reduce federal spending and let responsible citizens manage their own lives. With it in place, or at least imagined, we can turn our attention to those citizens who don't earn enough to meaningfully contribute to their own old-age saving, or even to obtain adequate food and shelter, but who have the potential for independence.

The main obstacle faced by potentially but not actually employable people is that they have been unable to develop the skills, vision, and motivation needed for success in the modern economy.[88] Or, while they might have useful skills, they have been unable or unwilling to connect with available job openings. While "job training" programs abound, they don't seem effective in bringing potential clients up to speed.

Here's a different approach. It's not wholly new but has a new twist that could make it effective.

Direct Assistance in Kind Rather than Cash or Subsidy

The cash payment model for public assistance is presumably predicated on the belief that individuals know best how to live their lives, lacking only money. This may not though be the case for people unsuccessful in planning and managing their lives. Assistance here should be in-kind and intended and structured as temporary life support and preparation for employment, not as a limited form of normal living. The safety net aspect provides basic food and shelter, without being an entitlement to a hammock that makes poverty tolerable. Working should always be more attractive.

Income problems are inherently personal. Effective assistance in solving them will also be personal and locally crafted. While nothing involving people is perfect, what seems to give the best results is personal coaching and direct assistance by individuals who actually know and care about their neighbors.

Responsibility must be at the state or local level. States and even large cities have different concepts of community responsibility. One virtue of our republic is that we have the power of a huge vibrant nation where it matters, and the diversity of local, regional and individual preferences where that is better suited to liberty, especially the part about not forcing others to believe as we do. A particular policy may be popular in one region but depreciated in another. We have the invaluable right to move from state to state. The argument that some states will provide inadequate assistance denies their people full citizenship. Diversity is strength.

If done by government this approach would be massive, impersonal, demeaning, costly and probably not conducive to its clients' self-improvement or even personal safety.[89] But there is a better way. Numerous charities do something of this nature right now at little expense and with compassion. They have volunteers and professional staff who work for little more than a sense of brotherly love or devotion to a religious or spiritual tradition.

Their common primary deficit is physical facilities in which to pursue their mission.

Leverage Charities

Government could provide, as a public good, suitable charities with physical facilities, utilities, insurance and bulk food, but not staff, and then get out of the way and let them do their good work. Don't worry if they want to preach their concept of god, as long as that doesn't include killing people who disagree with them. Exposing a few atheists to religion seems a small price to pay for also moving them from begging or welfare to productive work and responsible citizenship.

The Salvation Army and the Society of St. Vincent de Paul[90] are two of many examples that operate on a fairly large scale.

Homeboy Industries[91] in Southern California operates on a local scale from a religious origin.[92] It assists gang members and ex-convicts in turning their life around and joining mainstream society.

The independent Catholic Worker Houses around the country are an extreme example on a small scale.[93] They are run by anarchistic religious pacifists and might be difficult partners for a government agency but do good work at low cost. The endnote reference indicates that one of their major needs is buildings.

The Community First Village in Austin, Texas [94] provides not only simple homes but a range of counseling. As with the others, much of the work is done by volunteers, including residents. Also, their main need seems to be capital for facilities.

These non-governmental programs simulate, in an accelerated fashion, a home environment with real person-to-person mentoring in the ethos, motivation, and skills to succeed in today's labor market, and possibly also how to raise and support a family.

A Residential Learning Community

A facility where down and out and underemployed people can eat and sleep under the supervision of good-hearted mentors would be not only a cost-effective way to provide basic life support but should also ameliorate feelings of isolation and abandonment. A missing sense of community can be created. Such facilities would also bring clients to a common place where social workers and employment counselors could assist them in moving up the economic ladder. The connections formed in small-scale communal living could also facilitate mutual learning and assistance among the clients.

Employers needing low-cost labor might even find locating near a residential assistance facility could be better than going overseas, at least if burdensome regulations were relaxed.

A growing disincentive to employment is the alternative of claiming disability benefits.[95] This trend can be countered with professional mentoring by agencies that have successfully placed disabled people in work situations where they contribute and gain the respect of colleagues for doing what they can.[96] With close personal contact and compassion supported by suitable incentives both for clients and providers many people now living out of sight and just existing could enter or reenter the workforce. Again, government restrictions may need to be altered to encourage this kind of employment.

Employers today seek millions of workers. The available workers just aren't quite the right ones or in quite the right places.[97] Getting unemployed job seekers to where the jobs are is a problem[98] for which centralized government assistance may be a true public good justifying the cost of a moving van or a bus ticket. Job seekers with mortgages could be offered public assistance in untangling their real estate and possibly buying in the new location if the nature of the new job made success plausible.

Costs and Controls

The government need not provide much money directly to the service providers or their clients. Small amounts could, though, pay nominal stipends, not wages, to people who are at the same time clients and volunteer frontline workers such as part-time kitchen and cleaning staff.

As with any program that spends other people's money, auditing for results and costs is essential. Civil service auditors must learn how to relate to groups that are less organized than the typical business.

When a product or result is not subject to competition in an open market, the process can decay. This happened to a well-intentioned local community service agency in Southern Oregon that provided care and counseling to drug abusers and their families. When auditors finally looked closely they found extensive evidence of poor care, unknown results, and even abuse. The founding director of an operation that had earned a stellar reputation had to be terminated and festering problems corrected at great expense and interruption of client care.[99] Despite this, the results were probably better than had the government simply given money to the clients without such personal attention.

Those few clients found at intake or after well-considered attempts at personal growth to be unable to provide for themselves should be recognized as wards of the state and housed in group facilities where they can live in a humane safe environment similar to those discussed here but without the expectation of independent employment. The cost should be a blip compared to our present transfer programs.

Incentives

The most important factor in self-development is motivation, which can arise from internal drive or from external incentives. If the former is lacking, the latter must be provided. For clients, the incentives could be personal encouragement and recognition, or even tastier food or more comfortable quarters. This degree of individualized incentives would be difficult and probably illegal for a government agency but should be feasible for a private charity with close and continuing contact between counselors and clients in a residential setting.

The ranks and available time of charity workers could be expanded by finding a way for them to receive a share of the public benefits gained by transitioning clients from welfare to employment. For example, a counselor or mentor who successfully places a chronically unemployed or underemployed client in a job that generates income tax could be paid half of that tax as it is received over a period of years. In time, with multiple successful clients, this could become an appealing income stream. The mentor would have a real incentive to prepare and match clients to jobs with good long-term prospects. Note these payments come from new government tax revenue that is a net gain relative to the expense of providing income support.

This would be quite a departure from the present incentive for clerks in a welfare or unemployment office to maintain a large pool of clients. Any program has incentives. They just must be the right ones.

The program proposed here replaces direct payment to individuals with facilities and support systems that facilitate entry into the word of productive work. It can be considered a public good that contributes to the general welfare much like public schools. It is not an entitlement. The costs can be budgeted by a regular appropriation process, not automatic spending. A multiplicity of small projects will be complex, but amenable to evaluation by pilot programs, unlike the failing programs that must be replaced. Prudence also requires that any changes to the existing programs be gradual to accommodate the many people dependent on them.

The Economy

Governments at federal, state, and local levels attempt to manage our economy. Why? What does that even mean? What should be the objectives? What is the difference between supporting, promoting, regulating, and managing? Should government do any of these things? How does this affect liberty?

Essential Support

Much of America's success in creating a bountiful life compared to other times and other countries is due to government policies and actions. Those that directly support a vibrant, productive economy include

- a commonly accepted and reasonably stable currency
- a safe and sound banking system
- a legal system that
  - helps market participants make stable, enforceable, and meaningful contracts and transactions, and
  - provides relatively good security in property and one's person
- a huge national market
  - accessible to anyone who can create a desired product, and that
  - provides a vast range of opportunities for employment and entrepreneurship
- an adequate physical infrastructure
- Education and research

These public goods support economic activity, contributing to the general welfare. They are neutral and non-discriminatory because they create an environment in which individuals can conduct business at their own pace and direction to their individual benefit, which aggregates into a general benefit. No one is singled out and required to do anything, incur a specific cost, or receive a unique benefit. The lack of such public goods distinguishes poor backward nations from prosperous ones.

Counterproductive "Help"

The downside is that government power sufficient to provide these benefits, plus all the others discussed in this chapter, tempts officials to imagine they have more power than they really do, and can make constituents' lives better by tweaking a few economic factors. Targeted interest groups benefit. The cost isn't noticed if it is spread thinly enough over everyone else. The result, though, is a proliferation of laws, programs, officials, and grateful clients.

Examples abound. Here are a few that attempt to manage the economy

- Federal
  - Money supply and interest rates — to control the business cycle
  - Banking and credit regulations — Community Reinvestment Act[100, 101]
  - Import duties to protect domestic industries — e.g. sugar and steel
  - Subsidies and tax credits — solar, wind, electric cars, foreign sales guarantees, extraction of natural resources[102]
  - Income tax deductions — home mortgage interest, charitable contributions, depreciation
  - Differential tax rates on income — capital gains vs. earned, carried interest,[103] non-profits
  - Mandate (with fines) to buy health insurance[104]
- State
  - Temporary tax relief to entice new companies
  - Government sales assistance (often overseas), tourism promotion
  - Subsidies for favored industries — solar, mass transit
- Local
  - Enterprise zones (low tax, subsidized infrastructure)
  - Eminent domain acquisition of land for private development[105]

- o Monopoly franchises — utilities, taxicab permits, transit lines
- o Direct subsidies — mass transit, arts

These two sets of policies are very different.

The first set has government non-coercively providing a supportive environment (a good definition of the general welfare), while the second has government guiding or forcing individual actions, or even taking property for the private benefit of another.

There is a small but important area between these two types of policy where there is a role for government to maintain the freedom and openness of markets. While contentious and dependent on judgment and sometimes arcane logic, the object of antitrust law is to prevent economic sclerosis or harm to consumers caused by "excessive" industrial concentration. It is not a major factor in either liberty or our economy so will not be pursued further here.

The first set of policies account for a minuscule part of government spending and clearly qualify as supporting the general welfare. The Constitution specifically grants the federal government power to regulate the currency, set standards for weights and measures, and enforce contracts. The argument that these enumerated powers are obsolete because our technology and economy have developed far beyond anything imagined in 1787 is specious. For example, antibiotics and other modern medicines were not even imagined then but setting standards to at least quantify and publish if not control their safety and efficacy is a reasonable extension of these powers granted in eighteenth-century terms.

The federal government is granted the power to regulate commerce between the states and with foreign nations. The purpose is to foster a national market and prevent states from imposing duties or other undue restrictions on such commerce.

This power has been extended to regulate virtually all aspects of commerce.

How did we allow the federal government to grow its power from providing an environment conducive to a vibrant economy to actually managing that economy, sometimes in risible detail as when a farmer was fined for raising a few acres of wheat for his own animals? [106] The Federal Reserve System is representative of several agencies that were created with sound constitutional justification but that have expanded their reach from supporting the economy to attempting to manage it.

The Role of the Federal Reserve

A reliable currency is a prime example of a public good and how the concept can be corrupted. A stable, credible currency promotes the general welfare by facilitating a productive economy. People can exchange wealth more conveniently and safely by using money than by, for example, trading a sheep for a dental filling. Storing wealth over time this way is also more practical for the same reason. For the value of money to be stable, the quantity available in the economy must match the amount of goods and services available for exchange, which for a healthy economy usually increases, but always fluctuates. Managing this credibly can be complex and uncertain, but creating new money should require an effort commensurate with the money's nominal value.

In the US, the Federal Reserve System manages the money supply. They must determine how much new real wealth is being created to justify the creation of new money, and how to inject that new money into the economy. The Fed does this, in part, by monitoring reams of economic data and by providing newly created money to banks for lending to borrowers. For example, a builder borrows this money to construct a house and then repays the bank when the house is sold, allowing the bank to re-lend the money to new borrowers. The new money created this way is matched first by the builder's credible promise to repay, and ultimately by the value of the newly constructed house.

This is how the system is supposed to work. The Federal Reserve though must exercise considerable judgment and discretion throughout the process, which therefore is subject to errors in execution and to political interference.

The Great Depression

Federal attempts to correct supposed deficiencies in the economy started at the end of an unexceptional economic boom in the late 1920s when stock market prices crashed after rising to levels unsupported by the real economy. This crash was a disaster for the tens of thousands of Americans holding stocks but would not have affected the real economy of the other hundred million except for a fatal mistake of the newly established Federal Reserve System. The story is complicated,[107] but briefly, the Fed caused the Great Depression of the 1930s by reducing the money supply when they should have increased it. They used their new power of regulating the currency to match the reduction in value of stocks when they should have increased it to counteract the banks' necessary reduction in their lending due to the same reduction in assets. Experts differ, but in hindsight, while the economic crash (not the market crash) could have been prevented by a modest Fed intervention in the right direction, the US would have been better off had the federal government done nothing.

Conflicting Goals

This lesson was not learned in time and is still subject to debate because of the complexity and obscurity of the process. There remains a belief that there can be public or at least political benefit from manipulating the money-creation process to gain the utility of new wealth without backing up the new money with real wealth. Since 1978, the Federal Reserve has been directed to manage US currency with not just one difficult goal but with two conflicting goals—stable prices and full employment. (Humphrey-Hawkins Full Employment Act of 1978)[108] The goal of stable prices, while difficult, is a technical possibility. Full-employment, however, while a laudable wish, is neither a granted power nor a goal that can realistically be achieved by government action in a nation of liberty. The problem is that trying to achieve full employment by currency manipulation weakens the value of that currency. This is evident in the current policy of purposefully manipulating the quantity of money to cause a 2% annual decrease in the purchasing power of the US dollar.[109] This not only distorts the economy, forcing users of dollars to continually adapt to their debasement but infringes on liberty by imposing a hidden tax on those of modest means for whom saving cash is the only practical way to accumulate wealth.

Even though much of what the Federal Reserve does is an overreach of authority, calls to abolish it[110] are premature[111] until it is assigned a single mandate to manage the currency for constant purchasing power, and is given the opportunity to succeed at that.

Erosion of Privacy

Creation and management of money can be a crucial element of the general welfare, but there are risks to liberty when a government goes beyond providing that service to prying into and controlling the lives of citizens. Governments around the world are moving to augment or even replace cash with digital banking via credit or debit cards.[112] Customers find it convenient, and banks significantly reduce the costs of many kinds of transactions. This is fine except that governments have discovered that by moving transactions from cash to digital, and themselves controlling the process, they can monitor all the transactions of their citizens. The stated purpose is to restrain tax evasion.[113] But the temptation to use this information to control transactions or for other purposes will be too much to resist. Our constitution denies government the power to compel a person to testify against himself. This freedom will be lost. Liberty requires the government to be a servant of the people, not their mother or their conscience.

Managing Markets

Academics and other curious people naturally want to know how the world works. Economics is the science of observing, measuring, and describing how people interact in exchanging goods and services.

Expert Economists

The problem with expert economists is that while they share a body of more or less accepted knowledge about many technical aspects of the subject, they disagree about applying it to the real world. This means that most of the time, half of them are wrong. Paul Krugman, Milton Friedman, and Friedrich Hayek all received Nobel Prizes in economics,[114] and John Maynard Keynes would have except he died before the prizes were awarded. These men are all widely recognized as experts, yet they express opposite opinions on fundamental aspects of economic policy. Keynes and Krugman think they understand national economies well enough to manage them. Friedman sort of agrees but thinks those two got the process wrong. Hayek doesn't think it's possible or even desirable. His argument is the best because he recognizes the hubris of central control and the value of liberty.

Economic gurus offer advice comporting with their own principles, believing they have discovered a lever by which to make things better. For example, if a significant number of people seem unable to afford an adequate standard of living, they recommend passing a law to mandate these people be paid more. If not enough people buy homes, they support a banking regulation requiring more mortgages be issued to specified types of people. If a city or state seems to need more jobs, arrange to subsidize a business that will build a factory there.

We are then shocked when retired people lose their purchasing power to inflation or higher taxes, or markets freeze up and people lose real jobs and real houses. What happened? Who is to blame? Could it possibly have been the well-intentioned but misguided policies supposed to help people?

John Allison[115] draws on his inside experience to show how free markets correct their own problems and lead to long-term prosperity, whereas trying to nudge them with direct government "help", as opposed simply to providing public goods, is a losing proposition.

Industrial Support

Supporting export industries seems like a good idea. It puts people to work and brings money into the US. One way to do this is to provide government guaranteed financing to foreign airlines to buy aircraft from American manufacturers, like Boeing in Seattle. This guarantee allows a foreign airline to borrow money at a rate lower than it would otherwise have to pay on the open market, which motivates it to buy from Boeing rather than, say, Airbus in France. The airline eventually repays the loan, so the guarantee isn't invoked and it doesn't cost our government anything. Everyone wins, right?

Not quite. US domestic airlines must pay the full market price for loans to buy aircraft, so their ticket prices must be slightly higher than those of the foreign airline that received the preferential deal. These can then undercut US airlines in the international travel market. The effects are small but apply to many airlines over the life of their planes. The result is fewer ticket sales and therefore fewer employees at the domestic airlines. The jobs saved at Boeing were concentrated and visible, but those lost at domestic airlines are too diffuse and obscured by all the other factors of business to be attributed to the export subsidy.[116] Then Airbus gets a similar subsidy from the French government to entice American airlines to buy planes from them rather than from Boeing, so even the visible gain of jobs vanishes.

The Mirage of Central Planning

These examples illustrate some general truths. The first is that central planners can never obtain enough information to foresee even the main effects of an intervention in a market. There are too many factors and they interact in too many ways, none of which are perfectly understood. Even if planners somehow could gather all the relevant information for one time, the known uncertainties and complexity of trade would make deriving a plan for the future impossible.

The second reason central planners can never fine-tune an economy is that it's made of people, not machines or computer programs. People follow different dreams and have different values, some of which they don't even understand very well themselves, and of which distant planners have no clue.

Finally, whole new technologies, business models, and social trends will continue to upset any overall plan, no matter how well-intentioned or crafted. Then there are grand mistakes and selfish motives, especially in the real world.

The beauty of a free society and its economy is that central planning is unnecessary. Whether it could "work" or not, the cost to gather and analyze all the data would be enormous, as would, or are, the control mechanisms. These costs are an added overhead or burden on the productive economy, reducing its useful output. A market economy does all this within itself by using the information distributed for free by prices.

How Do You Make a Pencil?

A classic illustration is the realization that no one knows how to make something as simple as a wooden lead pencil. By no one, I mean no one person, company, or agency. Sure, the pencil company knows how to shape, assemble and wholesale them, but they don't know how to grow and harvest the trees for the wood, or mine the graphite for the "lead", or how to obtain and process the material that goes into the paint. They probably don't know how to mine the metals used to make the dies that stamp the labels on the sides of the pencil. At the other end of the process, they probably would not be very good at running the retail stores that sell them to the public, or the trucks that deliver them to the stores.

The figurative army that provides us with pencils consists of thousands of people who mostly don't even know each other, much less cooperate actively. They all obtain just enough information from their proximate cooperators by knowing the prices each demand for their products and services. Furthermore, in most cases, they know of several competing sources or customers and buy or sell based on many factors such as price, availability, and reputation for quality.

Try to imagine a central commissar for national pencil production attempting this. Oh wait, we don't need to imagine it. It's been tried.[117]

These truths are well described and explained by the noted economist Friedrich Hayek in his popular book, *The Road to Serfdom*.[118] It is must reading for anyone considering government management of an economy. Its strength lies in its consideration of people and their interactions as they are, much of which is unknowable, not as they uniformly and ideally might be. Hayek is an excellent source for the principles and consequences of central planning, but he must be read in the context of his era, which included the Soviet Union and state ownership of the means of production. Modern progressives have learned a little bit from this and so rarely try to have the government actually own factories, farms, and retail stores. They just want to impose enough rules and regulations on them to have the benefits of control without the responsibility of ownership. The result is the same.

Cost Burden
These are the economic results of central planning. The damage to respect for government, social comity, personal equanimity and liberty is worse. Most businesses and individuals see most of their decisions dependent in some way on federal rules. These have an inordinate impact on success or failure, so people in business are motivated to exert as much influence as possible through the political process, including spending money. Thousands of highly-paid lobbyists are registered in Washington DC, constituting an estimated $9 billion industry by

themselves.[119] No amount of rules restricting such spending will prevent this. It will just appear in different guises. For individuals who can't exert significant influence on the government, the result is a continuous state of tension over the direction of their lives reflected in hypersensitivity to election results.

The challenge, or conflict, is that the government must remember* its job is to protect the liberty of the people while managing a very large enterprise organized along top-down authoritarian principles. Government leaders are in charge of millions of armed troops, vast stretches of public lands, enormous sums of money, our nation's borders and more. These must be managed based on centralized responsibility, and the tendency is to carry this mindset over to broader social issues including the economy. The people should not be managed, though that is a natural result when many want government favors or support.

There is no doubt that a centrally planned command economy could be managed by an army or other authority. Everyone would have a job and know his duties. Part of the Egyptian economy has been run this way for decades, but the result is neither a strong economy nor liberty. [120] There is no evidence this is a good idea for any length of time. Winning WWII was a four-year triumph of top-down leadership and national unity. We had a mortal enemy, a clear objective, and a definite endpoint. When it was over, we shut down the effort. Putting men on the moon was a purely technical industrial program supported by an almost invisible level of extra taxation. It required no special effort, participation, or commitment from most citizens. Managing the whole economy and providing permanent income support to most people have nothing in common with these projects. There is no clear objective and no end point. Federal programs exert control over major factors in everyone's life and incur vast and increasing expense forever.

---

* Government is actually able to remember. It is made of legislators, administrative officials, consultants and judges who have made it their career, whether in or out of office.

Taxes

Liberty doesn't come without cost. A strong government protects against domestic and foreign forces that would physically attack us. Armies, police, and fire departments are expensive and must be maintained in readiness to respond when needed, not later. Fulfilling the mission to promote the general welfare also incurs substantial costs. The best source for these funds is taxes.

Be Glad You Have to Pay Taxes

Taxes are not a necessary evil — having to pay them can help preserve liberty. Needing to obtain voters' approval for imposing taxes is a powerful mechanism for citizens to retain control over government. When English kings could not fund their rule from their own extensive lands, they were forced to accede to the demands of powerful barons and grant them the right to approve the king's taxes.[121]

Governments being able to self-fund — that is, rule with no taxes, perhaps by exploiting abundant natural resources or owning factories — sounds nice at first, but commonly leads to corruption and despotism.[122, 123] The oil-rich Arab states in the Persian Gulf are not only able to self-fund from energy exports, they subsidize their citizens' living expenses. And they all exemplify an almost complete lack of liberty.

Norway and the State of Alaska seem to be exceptions, but the first already had a long history of responsible government, and Alaska is well integrated into the American system.

A telling example of a different kind of government failure caused by self-funding is provided by several counties in Southwest Oregon that at one time supported most of their services by royalties on sales of timber from federal forests. Over the past thirty years or so these timber sales have been severely reduced, leading to major budget shortfalls. The taxpayers in some of these counties, having become accustomed to unusually low property taxes, have refused to vote for increases to make up for the lost timber revenue, with the result that services have been sharply curtailed.[124] As is usually the case, the most popular services, such as police protection, suffer the most.

Paying taxes, therefore, is not only necessary; it can be a way for citizens to control government, even if unwisely. This connection between taxation and taxpayer influence on government has, however, been weakened or lost in many ways.

Corruption of the Power to Tax

Article I, Section 8 of the US Constitution grants Congress the power to "lay and collect taxes" and to "make all laws which shall be necessary and proper for carrying into execution the foregoing (enumerated) powers, and all other powers vested by this Constitution in the government of the United States".

These two principles seem to restrict the federal government to just those powers that are explicitly granted, or in its terms, enumerated. Taken together, they and the Tenth Amendment are abundantly clear that taxes may be imposed only to support such powers.

Control via Taxation

Unfortunately, considering only the first phrase in isolation, some argue that Congress is granted essentially unlimited power to tax without having to be very specific about how the subsequent spending is authorized by its enumerated powers. The result is that Congress has been able to exert substantial control over the states by collecting more tax than is necessary to fund its enumerated powers, and then giving this money back to the states, and sometimes directly to individuals, on the condition they obey a rule that Congress does not have the authority to pass as a law.

One example is the "Helmet Law". There is little question that wearing safety helmets is a good idea for motorcycle riders. There is, however, nothing in the US Constitution that even with broad interpretation grants Congress the power to require motorcycle riders to wear helmets. (This has nothing to do with there being no motorcycles when the Constitution was adopted). Congress has, however, conditioned receipt of federal funds for road construction (a legitimate power) on states enacting helmet laws.

The federal government has no authority to prohibit alcoholic beverages or tobacco products. But it has unlimited power to tax them, and to jail people for evading the tax. It can, therefore, set the tax high enough to discourage smoking or drinking, which it has no power to do by means of a direct law.

Congress is not authorized to force us to buy electric cars. Purely aside from the argument that they're a good thing, the federal government is granted no such power and doesn't try to put you in jail for not buying one. But, it can refund an unlimited amount of the income tax you pay if you do buy one.

The same principle allows the federal government to impose controls on schools. It is not granted any power to manage schools, but it gives them money. This money is then conditioned on acceding to rules that Congress would not otherwise be empowered to enact as law.

Mandates Equated to Taxes

A much more important example is the requirement imposed by the Affordable Care Act (Obamacare) on every citizen to buy a health insurance policy or pay a special penalty. By calling this penalty a tax, and believing Congress is empowered to levy a tax for any purpose, The Supreme Court was able to justify and approve a power that it recognized was not granted. [125, 126, 127]

These are all examples of government trying to make you act as though you believed some particular idea by manipulating the tax you must pay. Invoking the General Welfare clause does not authorize this practice because it expresses a purpose of the Constitution, not an enumerated grant of power.

Good laws tell you what you may not do. Bad laws tell you what you must do. Using taxes to "nudge" or encourage people is just that, hidden behind the power to tax.

Liberty demands that the taxing and spending power of the federal government not be exploited to extend federal authority beyond the powers explicitly enumerated in the Constitution. Specifically, the federal government must stop using grants of money or tax relief to coerce states and citizens into following "guidelines" that the federal government has no legitimate power to impose.

Whom to tax

"Don't tax you, don't tax me. Tax that fellow behind the tree."
Senator Russell B. Long.[128]

The question is not whether to impose taxes or even how high they should be. That's just a matter of priorities and costs. The hard question is how to apportion taxes among the citizens. Then there's the question of the purpose of taxation. Is it simply to raise enough money to support the operation of government, or is it to achieve some other end? This is too big a subject to consider here in any depth, but let's take a brief look at some of the main issues from the perspective of liberty.

Beneficiaries

As a general proposition, it sounds reasonable to require those who benefit from a government service to pay for it. Fuel taxes to support road building are a good example. Supporting property services such as fire protection by taxing property based on its value would be another. But a different approach is also possible.

Ability to Pay

Ability to pay also sounds on its face to be a reasonable criterion in part because it is a plausible proxy for the benefit received from liberty and those services and facilities that constitute general welfare. The owner of large tracts of land or factories may well benefit more than a person with no property or other wealth or income. Thus, local governments usually tax property proportionally to its market value. Another natural proxy for ability to pay is, of course, income.

An extreme version from the early part of the past century expressed a similar principle with a simple-to-understand slogan: *From each according to his ability to each according to his need.* [129, 130] It's easy to discern this principle in our current policy of taxation based on ability to pay, and benefits based on need, but when practiced in its original form, it hasn't worked out well. Unfortunately, this lesson has been ignored.

Basing policy on Karl Marx's slogan has transformed taxation from supporting the government in an equitable way to using it for larger goals, such as:

Income or wealth equalization

A tax where the rate itself increases with income equalizes income. It's called progressive both because of the progression of the rate with income but also because it supports the principles of Progressivism. It usually means that people with relatively low income pay no tax while there is no limit to the highest rate. It, therefore, has the potential to severely limit liberty. Another negative result of progressive tax rates is that when a schedule has been in effect for a while, any future flattening in the rates can be attacked as a gift to the wealthy because they already pay at a higher rate.

Taxation without representation is an obvious injustice and led to the American Revolution.[131] Representation without taxation is just as insulting to liberty. Every citizen should pay at least some tax so he or she feels responsible for the government. This is probably better than conditioning representation, or voting, on paying any particular tax because the universal franchise is a bulwark of aspects of liberty that extend well beyond taxation. Still, allowing people to vote on taxes they know will never apply to them seems wrong.

Influencing people's choices and decisions

A particularly pernicious affront to liberty is to employ the tax process to "encourage" citizens to do or not do things that the government otherwise has no legitimate power to control, or to curry favor with certain voters. For its first century, the federal government could favor certain products, and therefore producers, by adjusting import duties and taxes on luxuries like whiskey, as there was hardly any income tax until 1913.[132, 133] We now have an industry of highly paid professionals who help larger taxpayers navigate the 75,000 pages[134] of federal tax law to structure their business and personal lives to at least nominally bend to the central planning desires of Congress and state legislatures.

Are you "asked" to pay them?

Using taxes to shift the cost of government from a large group of voters to a smaller group of other voters is exemplified by the oft-heard appeal to "ask" some to pay a "fair" share that is higher than imposed on the first group. Ignoring the impossibility of objectively defining "fair" in this context (beyond simply "more"), there is still the corruption of language in characterizing a demand backed by armed men and jails as "asking". Remember, one of the rules of liberty is I don't take the property of others. The implication is I don't take it for my own use. Much of taxation is just that.

Small Nuisance Taxes

A small subchapter in the long story of continually nibbling away at citizens' property is the proliferation of small charges added to many automatic transactions. These charges aren't called taxes but are money deftly lifted from our pockets for purposes we only dimly understand and over the spending of which we have no effective control. Look at your telephone or utility bill and see if you can explain all the little amounts like the Universal Service Fund, the Franchise fee or Federal Regulatory Recovery. Have our elected representatives debated these, and do they evaluate the results of spending them? Do they even know what they are?

Can Federal Taxes be Reduced?

Conservative politicians campaigning for federal office often promise to reduce the federal tax burden by returning responsibilities to the states. This might once have been possible, but the federal debt is now so large[*] that federal taxes must remain at their present level for decades even if some responsibilities are reverted to the states and the annual federal budget shows a surplus, just to pay off past debt. (There is an alternative. The federal government could inflate the currency so much that the debt, which is in fixed dollars, would be easy to pay. The cost would be borne by people of modest means who have no realistic options for saving except in dollars, which would be devalued).

The Decline of Taxes as a Limit on Government

Taxes used to be an important check on government overreach. In the 1767 Townsend Acts, King George III imposed a modest tax on the American colonies without their consent. This eventually led to the American Revolution, by which the King lost those colonies. In 1988 President George H. W. Bush famously promised "No New Taxes", but his later acquiescence to some modest increases lost him the next election.

Those were the days when governments had to collect taxes to at least approximately pay for their spending. They could borrow money, but they and their citizens expected to eventually pay it back. Governments, and the citizens who elect them have recently discovered marvelous tricks to avoid this limitation. The result is that reluctance to pay taxes no longer limits government spending. And when government spending mostly pays income support to individuals, the potential for buying the allegiance of

---

[*] $20,000,000,000,000 and counting.

134

voters is unlimited. Remembering the liberty rule of not cheating or tricking people, here are some of these tricks:

Inflate the Currency

An old one that doesn't work well anymore is to inflate, that is debase, the currency. If the government borrows $1000, it promises to repay that $1000 in, say, ten years plus perhaps 2% annual interest. The trick was that it also inflated the currency by 2% in each of those ten years so that the $1000 it repays buys only 82% of what the money bought when borrowed. The government also collected income taxes on the 2% the lender received. Knowledgeable lenders eventually caught on and weren't as eager to buy bonds anymore. (Did you know that the official policy of the Federal Reserve is to manage the money supply so there is 2% inflation each year? [135] Saving dollars is a sucker's game).

Plan to Never Repay Debt

A recently developed trick is to borrow money with no intent of collecting the taxes that would be necessary to repay it. That way the government can spend as much as it wants without the taxpayers revolting and voting them out of office. The money available to please voters or fight a war is almost unlimited. Today the United States owes twenty trillion dollars and no politician of either major party has a credible plan to repay it. (Some of this debt is owed to real people, and some is simply borrowed from the Fed which creates it out of thin air, but these are details).

Do you know what twenty trillion dollars is? It's more than we produce in goods and services in a whole year. To pay it back we would all need to do our same work all year and neither eat nor have a place to live during that time. Not likely. Don't ask what happens. I don't know, but it can't end well. Little countries like Greece can just go bankrupt, and everyone who has loaned them money loses some. I think it's worse for big countries like America. The US dollar being an international reserve currency helps put off the reckoning but may make it more sudden and painful when it happens.   No one really knows.

Promise Unrealistic Benefits

A fairly new but more obscure trick for buying votes without raising taxes is to promise future benefits without having the means to pay for them. The trick comes in two versions. In the first, the promise is to pay unrealistically generous retirement benefits to government employees, who then vote for the elected officials making the promises. There are enough government employees to make a difference in elections, and they are very motivated. The State of Oregon is feeling the effects of this trick now. Its courts, where the judges are state employees, have ruled that legislative attempts to reduce some of the more egregious future employee benefits are illegal because they would violate the terms of an implied (by the judges) contract. Since Oregon can't inflate the currency or borrow without limit, it is forced to reduce services to make good on these promises.

The other version of the promise trick is to make similar but less binding promises to the citizens at large for future entitled benefits (Social Security, Medicare, Obamacare), which though ill-defined and not supported by taxes, are attractive enough to garner votes today, which is what matters to a politician.

Force Purchase of an Overpriced Product

The newest trick is to force some citizens to buy a product, such as health insurance, at an inflated price while offering the same product to others at a discounted price or free. The latter are grateful, and the process is obscure enough that the hidden tax is difficult to identify. The expense never appears in the federal budget or the national debt because it is paid directly by citizens. The proponents can claim to be fiscally responsible while scamming their subjects.

There really is a free lunch, at least for a while. Good luck, millennials.

Is There Hope for Reform?

British Prime Minister Margaret Thatcher[136] once pointed out "The problem with socialism is you eventually run out of other people's money."

What are the political implications of recognizing these tricks? We first must ask whether we care. Are we willing to forgo the pleasures of living on credit? Would we rather just toss the eventual crash to our children? If we are willing to suffer the pain of paying off our debts and living less high on the hog, how are we to do it? What huge changes to federal spending will we accept?

The difficulty can be seen in a proposal by The Manhattan Institute's Brian Riedl.[137] Reductions in entitlements and increases in taxes well beyond anything previously experienced will be necessary to even stabilize the increase in debt if we insist on retaining our present extra-constitutional programs.

Are there any political leaders who will be the adults, and put our nation back on a sustainable spending path?

I suggest one way to start is to reflect on the principles of liberty and the powers granted, and not granted, to the federal government by the Constitution. We need to stop lying to and tricking ourselves as shown in the preceding paragraphs. When we do this and realize we are spending well beyond our means, we must take hard looks at how we can stop borrowing and promising more than taxes can deliver. We should press our representatives for specific plans to make major reductions in the big spending categories. This means tackling entitlements. We can't say "Cut spending, but don't touch my Medicare." Obamacare is an obvious target, but it's not the whole problem.

A special tax to protect liberty

History shows that extreme concentration of property leads to a similar concentration of political power, or to just brute force, which tempts those possessing it to violate the rules of liberty. Taxation of extreme inherited wealth is an obvious means of preventing such a state of affairs. The death, or estate tax as presently imposed is, though, nothing more than a means to take someone else's property based on envy.

A legitimate death tax would prevent extreme concentration of multigenerational wealth. The specific risk from such concentration is monopoly denial of participation in free and open markets, and usurpation of government power. As far as I know, this principle has never been explicitly stated, much less supported by factual data and objective analysis. Relevant examples might be found in pre-revolutionary France, oil-rich Arabian Gulf monarchies, recently liberated African countries and Latin American banana republics. Such a tax would not be based on egalitarianism, or to raise significant revenue, but would be tailored to protect liberty itself.

An Ideal General Tax

I'll end this discussion of taxes by suggesting an ideal general tax. It should be:

- Roughly proportional to the ability to pay
- Visible to those paying it
- Evenly spread over the economy
- Free of compliance effort on the part of most citizens
- As progressive as the legislature may decide
- Neutral or positive in its effect on economic decisions by citizens
- Reliably collectible at a low administrative cost

Such a policy would replace all income taxes by a broadly-based national tax applied to all purchases of goods and services that could be enjoyed or consumed by an individual, but with exemptions supporting a basic standard of living. It would look at things rather than people. Envy would not be a factor.

The rate would have to be about 20% for the federal portion to replace current income tax revenue. It would exempt basic food, low-cost housing and cars, public transportation and goods bought at thrift stores. It would include all other housing and real estate purchases and rentals. It would include services such as lawyers, life coaches, and house painters. It probably should include all but the most basic medical services. It would not be applied to things people cannot consume, like stocks or bonds. Most people working for a salary or hourly wages would never need to file a return. They wouldn't even need to be known to the federal government unless they wanted a passport for foreign travel.

Businesses would pay the tax on everything they buy, except employee services. (Remember, there is no income tax). They would collect and remit the tax on everything they sell but could remit that tax in part with receipts for the tax they paid on their purchases. In this way, it would be like the European Value Added Tax (VAT) but much broader. The tax would be visible on retail receipts, reminding people of what they are paying for government.

Internet sales could be taxed now in the same manner. Rather than trying to allocate them to the state of the buyer, just let them go to the state of the seller, like any sales tax. This concept is currently in flux, with a recent Supreme Court decision[138] opening the door, but not very clearly. (This case is a good example of why such decisions should be made by legislatures rather than by courts.)

There would be complexities just as with our income tax system, but they would be of concern only to businesses and should be less than at present because there would be no rules about income or depreciation. Gifts would not be taxed and they would be real gifts, not just a way to avoid taxes. Charitable giving would be easier because there would be more disposable income. There would be fuzzy areas like how to tax what a wealthy person pays his butler or how to tax luxury goods privately imported, but these would be no worse than similar problems with our present system and apply to many fewer people. We would still need an IRS, but probably smaller, to administer the process.

This is only a hint at how our tax system could be made more compatible with the principles of liberty. Such a major change obviously warrants much more thought before being seriously considered.

Government Operation

The people hire government to perform certain tasks. How it goes about its business can be as important as the specific laws it enacts.

We spend a lot of money on government, and yield some of our freedom so the process can work. We recognize that the people at large cannot and should not involve themselves in every act of government, but we do need to choose goals and objectives and know how these are being met.

How can we achieve this?

Quality Control

The first step is to establish clear connections between objectives and the means of achieving them. Then, assess how the objectives are being met. That is, make sure that whatever process or program government undertakes is based on a rational understanding of cause and effect and actually achieves the purpose for which it was enacted. We can't let hope and mendacity replace honest assessment and analysis.

Take a lesson from manufacturing.

A product is designed with the intent to have certain features and attributes. The degree to which it meets measurable objectives for these is called *quality*, and the process of making, analyzing, and responding to the measurements is called *quality control*. (This is a mechanistic meaning of quality, not quite the same as beauty or desirability.) Applying something like this to government can help us evaluate and direct it.

We must know what we are trying to accomplish through government, and how closely that is being achieved. Legislative bills and administrative regulations should include quantitative objectives for both direct and foreseeable indirect results, both positive and negative. There will usually be disagreement about what these are.

Legislative objectives and anticipated results should be prepared quantitatively by both proponents and opponents and be formally part of the adoption process. They should include time schedules and costs. Budgets should include funds and means for quantitatively assessing the results over a time commensurate with the objectives.

In manufacturing, quality assurance includes analysis of failures to achieve the desired results. Causes are identified and the process is altered to correct them. If the desired results cannot be achieved at an acceptable cost, the product is abandoned (recalled). The same logic applies to government programs.

Good intentions are not enough. No program should be authorized simply to "address" a problem. There should be measurable goals. If these aren't met, a reason must be identified, and specific changes made to correct the failure. If after a certain number of tries there is no improvement, the program should be terminated.

Some states are trying to develop a form of quality control.[139] The federal government should try even harder because it spends more money.

Fix Causes, Not Symptoms

A refinement of quality principles is that product deficiencies are best corrected directly rather than covered up by add-on components. For example, if the front end in a new automobile design shimmies, it is better to find and fix the cause of the unbalance rather than just dampen out the vibration. In government, poor past policies should not justify worse new ones.

One example should be sufficient to make the point. The *Emergency Medical Treatment and Active Labor Act* (EMTALA) of 1986[140] requires hospitals to provide emergency care for all.[141] This law replaced an earlier one (Hill Burton)[142] with similar goals, with neither providing public funding to cover the costs. The predictable result was that other charges had to increase, leading to a demand for universal socialized medicine covering everyone. While this is an oversimplified account of a complex matter, the point is that government would have been more honest had it faced the initial problem directly. If a free service is to be provided, then we should identify it and tax ourselves to pay for it.

Good practice, when faced with a "problem", would therefore first be to discover whether prior government action contributes to the problem and correct that before passing a new law.

Focus and Reinvigorate Congress

The power balance inherent in the division of the federal government into three formally equal branches protects liberty. Maintaining such a balance is not automatic, or easy. Congress is supposed to create all federal laws while the administration executes them, and the courts decide if they are being obeyed. For this to work, the law-making power must remain with Congress. Self-funding and self-perpetuating agencies are anathema and should be abolished. Congress should consider and enact all laws and appropriations rather than be required to void bad ones created by officials[143]. (The same argument applies to state governments.)

Over half the federal budget is on autopilot. Congress doesn't even have to vote on it. This is a self-imposed insult to our legislators.

To avoid tricking the public, legislators should evaluate and approve each significant measure on its own merits. Holding essential measures hostage to unrelated issues or slipping policy in under the cloak of more visible issues is juvenile behavior unworthy of our representatives. Thousand-page bills are an invitation to hoodwinking the citizenry, especially when they leave significant policy decisions to administrators. Each legislative bill should be compact and focused enough that all legislators and interested citizens can read and understand it well before it comes to a vote. Recent practice by both political parties makes a mockery of the legislative process.

Ethics in Administration and Campaigns

Government officials, in proportion to their responsibility and authority, must perform their duties with integrity and openness in conformance to statutory obligations and the principles of liberty. (No private email accounts for public business, no gifts of employment to former officials)

Election campaigns are not strictly speaking part of government, but they suggest how officials will govern if elected. They must be conducted with honesty, integrity, and respect for the intelligence of voters.

Chapter 7

Politics of Liberty

In the end, it's all politics.

Clear and Honest Discourse

For us as citizens to effectively guide policy, we must involve ourselves in the operation of government by exchanging and assessing policy ideas. The liberty rule about not lying to or tricking people is a good guide.

Political discourse means sharing ideas. (Here we use *political* in the higher and necessary sense, not as it's corrupted by campaign machinations.) We must share our ideas so policy can be crafted, or for the majority who don't actually write laws, evaluated. Policy is built on ideas or concepts that originate in the mind but can be shared or made into laws only when put into words.* Words are essential to distinguish one concept from another.

---

* This is strictly true only in a constitutional republic. In a kingdom or dictatorship, law is whatever the ruler, or perhaps the mob, says it is in any instance. This seldom works out well.

This sounds simple, but carelessness leads not just to confusion but application of government force to situations not contemplated by those who approved the law.

Carelessness is bad enough but slipping in language that can be interpreted later to mean more than the initial perceived intent is nothing less than legislative fraud.

For a concept to be shared meaningfully, actually shared, it must be nearly the same in the minds of the originator and recipient. This doesn't mean agreeing or accepting. It simply means understanding or knowing. Otherwise, the parties aren't talking about the same thing and may not even know it. It's easy for a word to be heard or read the same but using words so the concept in each mind is nearly identical takes discipline. The best way to do this is to assign each distinct concept its own word, or phrase, that identifies it clearly. Again, speakers and listeners need not agree that the concept is desirable or not, just what it is.

To explore this principle let's analyze *rights* vs. *entitlements*. These examples are chosen not to argue a specific policy, but to illustrate the importance of using accurate and appropriate words as tools for communication. If different policy is preferred, fine. Just be sure the words used to communicate it are clear enough so meanings can be shared and effectively discussed.

Rights vs. entitlements

Rights define the details of liberty in terms of freedom from restraint, usually by government. In the United States, we can speak or write on any subject, assemble in peaceful groups, or join a church of our choice without fear of punishment. Television cop shows teach us that if arrested, we have a right to remain silent. These are good examples, but what exactly does the concept of a *right* mean? (We can immediately set aside meanings such as *correct* and the opposite of *left* as normally being clear in context.) I propose that the useful meaning in public policy should be the *freedom to do something without hindrance or permission*. The emphasis is on what you may do. You are not required to do anything, but if you have a right to do something, go ahead, no one should be able to stop you.

Sometime in the mid-twentieth century though, a different concept began to be slipped in under the name of rights, either carelessly or to deceive. Rather than being a freedom to do something without hindrance, *rights* began to be applied to the concept that the holder of a right could take possession of something. The generally respected right to life becomes the right to possess food necessary to support life, which is an entirely different concept because it means that someone else must provide that food. The almost universal approval of the right to life is stretched to include an obligation on another person. A mundane example might be when a city by ordinance grants the right to keep up to two cats as pets. If I want to keep a cat, I need not ask permission. At the same time, no one is obliged to provide me with a cat.

We find ourselves trying to discuss two very different concepts while using the same word to identify them. We need a new word.

Fortunately, we have one, *entitlement.* A good definition is that *someone entitled to something can take, possess, or must be given that thing with no other action on his part.* He is entitled to it just by being present or by having some other attribute. For example, in some cultures throughout history, the eldest son was *entitled* to his father's estate. He didn't need to do anything beyond being the eldest son. Nobles were entitled to certain goods and services just because they were nobles. (Originally, they were expected to provide protection, but eventually, the entitlement became basically hereditary.) At its founding, American law did not look favorably on entitlements, emphasizing instead certain inherent rights.

Absent the requirement on someone else to do something, an entitlement is meaningless. A right, though, requires no one to do anything. All it does is enjoin a restriction or denial. *Not interfering* and *providing* are two entirely different things and can't be lumped into a single concept without destroying meaning and communication.

The thing that an entitlement requires someone else to do is an *obligation*. There can be no entitlement without a corresponding obligation. Honest discourse requires that the corresponding obligation be part of any conversation about an entitlement. Since an entitlement requires the transfer of something of value from one person to another, it also seems proper to require that to be defined. An open-ended and unlimited entitlement would seem to violate important rights, such as to one's life on the part of the one on whom the obligation is imposed.

So, we have three words to convey three distinct concepts. If I propose an entitlement, you know I'm not talking about a right, and we can get on with our discussion. This is not to say that any of these things is good or bad, only that to discuss them we need clear communication.

If anyone thinks these distinctions are tedious, pedantic or unnecessary, consider that governments run by educated people have entered into treaties having the force of law while grossly ignoring them. In one particularly egregious example, the United States along with many other States ratified a treaty called *The Universal Declaration of Human Rights*.[1] It opens with a recitation of rights such as life, liberty, and free speech which, while observed in some countries more in the breach than in practice, are at least clear in meaning. It moves on to Article 25 which states in part that

"Everyone has the right to a standard of living adequate for the health and well-being of himself and of his family, including food, clothing, housing, and medical care and necessary social services, and the right to security in the event of unemployment, sickness, disability, widowhood, old age or other lack of livelihood in circumstances beyond his control."

148

While this collection of intentions might serve as an objective for society or even a goal for a socialist regime, it shows either an ignorance of language or a willful intent to obfuscate the difference between right and entitlement and ignores the corresponding obligations. It's wishful thinking at best, and license for confiscation at worst.

Stolen Concepts

It is false advertising to sell a concept under the name of something else to steal the acceptance of that name while offering something materially different.[2] It cloaks one concept, possibly even hidden, in another to gain undeserved acceptance. Other examples of stealing the positive connotation of one concept to gain acceptance of another unmentioned one include using *insurance* to cloak ongoing normal expenses or publicly supported income transfers, and *investment* to cloak continuing operating expenses.

The point of this argument is a plea for truth in policy. If you want to create an entitlement, call it that. Clarify the obligations and argue on the merits. Don't try to avoid those arguments by claiming an entitlement while calling it a right. Be sure that concepts like *everyone,* as in everyone pays and everyone benefits, are clear, truthful, and appropriate.

To put these ideas into practice in a political discussion, whenever someone assigns a proposition a name that appears different from its essence deduced from some of the details, call for a point of order and demand clarification and accurate naming.

What could go wrong?

No political philosophy or system of government has lasted forever. The better ones evolve; the worst collapse. Governing for liberty is a work in progress. We can see the goal, but we know we have not reached it, though government of the sort defined by the US Constitution is the closest any society has ever come. Even so, it is presumptuous to believe that our idea of liberty based on popular consent is the final answer to the question of how to govern human society. What might bring down the US Constitution and its ideal of liberty? Or on a more positive note, how might it evolve for the better?

Liberty based on popular consent requires several things of the great majority of citizens:

- To know what liberty is, to value it and live by it.
- To be educated enough to understand the basics of government necessary to preserve liberty.
- To have the self-restraint to accept substantial differences in economic and status outcomes between people.

The first two requirements are based on education, both formal and informal. The informal part is absorbed in families and daily life working and interacting with others. The formal part depends on teachers. If they don't value or even understand liberty, they aren't likely to impart that to students.

A more serious deficit in education about liberty results from its success in supporting a prosperous economy. People can become so comfortable that they devote their attention to wealth, entertainment or personal pleasure and never consider the fundamentals of the society in which they live. They become prey to demagogues who promise them even more comfort at the expense of a liberty they don't appreciate. They are like fish in the ocean that are not aware of water.

The third requirement exposes an inherent flaw in democracy, namely that people can vote themselves an entitlement to the property of others. Even though our constitutional framers tried to make that difficult, no amount of constitutional restrictions can prevent this because constitutions are not self-enforcing. Citizens must realize that even though they have the potential to use government force to take the property of others, the long-term net result would be their own or their descendant's impoverishment.

Factional Interest

This tendency was understood by the Framers as *Interest.*[3] They recognized that people will have different interests and will try to gain an advantage not only by productive efforts but by forming *factions* to use government to advance their own or impede others' interests. This seems a permanent feature of human nature.

A general principle for reducing the impact of interest can be stated as *Government must be designed and maintained to maximize the influence of wisdom and minimize the influence of factional interest in making and enforcing laws.*

Like all principles, this contains a wealth of detail to be defined. It may even be too broad to be useful. Let's see.

- The Constitution attempts to reduce the impact of factional interest by diffusing government power between branches and even between parts of the branches. In our time
  - Has the legislature yielded too much power to the executive and judiciary? Can these power centers be captured by factional interest?
  - Has the federal government taken too much power from the states?
  - How have liberty and equity faired in this struggle?
- The influence of interest supposedly is minimized by universal suffrage, i.e. by more direct democracy.
  - But this assumes some common level of understanding, independence, and participation.
  - Can those who expect to receive and become dependent on the benefits of wealth sharing be independent and disinterested?

151

- o Currently, this effort focusses on majority voting in which argument is ideally conducted free from the use of wealth to publicize and mold opinions.
- o Can a majority vote ever establish sharing of wealth free of the influence of interest? Does it matter?
- Wisdom is sought by basing legislative power on other than pure democracy and by a lifetime judiciary.
  - o How is this working out?

There are no permanent answers to these questions. Continually seeking them is part of preserving liberty.

Improving political argument

Political argument provides a large part of the informal education about public affairs. There are claims and counterclaims about the effect of proposed policy choices. The citizens' task is to judge the integrity of competing claims based on limited factual knowledge, sometimes about the future but more often regarding generalities about people and their behavior. This requires humility and appreciation of the human differences underlying the value of liberty. Parents and K–12 teachers are probably the best situated for this, but again, if their understanding of liberty is flawed, how can they pass it on?

How to do this is beyond the scope of this book and my skills, but here are a few hints.

- Be suspicious of claims to make people's lives better through direct government action.
- Look for evidence that benefits to one come at the expense of another. Consider the effect on liberty.
- Hyperbolic rhetoric suggests a paucity of principles or ignorance of facts.
- Try to agree on the facts. Then debate principles and preferences. Know the difference.

- The larger the proposed program, the longer it should take to approve, and the larger should be the consensus.
- Be sure that everyone involved understands the details and ramifications of a proposal before approving it. This favors small proposals and concise laws limited to one issue.
- Retrieving an entitlement once granted is vastly harder than granting it, almost impossible.
- If a proposed law is too complex for the average person to understand, it is probably a bad idea.
- If it sounds too good to be true, it probably is.
- Rely more on the proven integrity of advocates than on their specific predictions.
- Integrity is not the same as delivering pork.
- When someone tells you to just trust him, run.
- Prefer small discrete improvements to wholesale new programs.
- Demand those operating government, from candidates to legislators to administrators, to be as clear, complete, and honest in their descriptions of conditions, policy, expectations, and results as possible.
- An expert in one subject, like entertaining, probably doesn't know any more outside that specialty than you do.
- Be wary of arguments presented in television commercials or "documentaries." They are well crafted to present only selected and unverified examples in a well-written storyline. You can't study them very well because they are transitory, unlike a book where you can examine individual statements.

There is no superior authority to enforce liberty. It's up to us.

Parties

This book rarely if ever mentions the Democratic, Republican, or even Libertarian party, which are essential to the practical work of organizing people to bring political ideas to the great majority of busy citizens.

The two major parties operate more on team spirit than philosophy and embody the principles discussed here to varying degrees and with more-or-less equal electoral success, dominating our political life.

The Libertarian Party has exhibited little electoral success, possibly because of its members' concentration on political theory and less on the practical governance issues treated here. The Cato Institute[4] is a fount of libertarian ideas[5] that sometimes find their way into the more general arena of political life.

To the extent these parties embody the principles of liberty, I salute them and encourage readers to join in their work.

It would be convenient to use the term "liberal" to refer to the principles of liberty or a person supporting them. Unfortunately, for obscure historical reasons, the term has shifted from that to mean Progressivism or just the Democratic Party.[6] Its usefulness has been degraded to where it's best to just let it go. Libertarian with a small "l" will have to do even though it's also the name of a party.

Advocates of liberty are at a political disadvantage compared to progressives because the latter like the idea of an active government, while libertarians along with some conservatives mostly just tolerate it. Progressives are more willing to devote their time and energy to a strong central government either as officials, activists or consultants because they believe it is the proper regulator of human affairs.

Chapter 8

Contrary Principles

Liberty has many competitors for regulating public affairs.

A multitude of alternative principles and government structures have been conjured to improve our public and private lives. Several have been insinuated into our nominally liberty-based government. Some are more contrary or hostile to liberty than others. Some are even complementary in certain aspects, but all are alternatives. They distinguish themselves from liberty by positing, and often enforcing, a distinct vision of the way people and their world should be. Liberty in contrast simply proposes a few restrictions on individual behavior, extends them to government, and does not otherwise require conformity of belief, behavior or result.

This chapter considers several alternative principles, in no particular order. Except for an occasional mention, extreme corruptions of governance such as totalitarianism and theocracy are not considered. We're interested in political philosophies that have been proposed or tried in America.

Egalitarianism

The egalitarian believes that no one should possess "too much" more material goods than anyone else. The question of what is too much is left unanswered except as justification for more confiscation. Egalitarianism should not be confused with the concept of equality before the law, that is, the equal right to liberty.

Since egalitarians decline to state just how much is too much, we assume they mean something like "Any amount of wealth or income greater than the median is really the property of the State" and therefore can be taxed away. This might be limited only by the realization that taking this much might be self-defeating. This is contrary to liberty and has no place in our republic.

Egalitarianism is the unstated principle behind graduated (progressive) income tax rates and luxury taxes. The principle is never subjected to objective analysis to justify particular tax rates or to learn the actual effects of such rates which are always set based on relative political power. Since a graduated tax rate imposes greater taxes on people with higher income, any proposed reduction in the upper rates is objected to on the grounds it provides greater benefits to the "rich," which it unavoidably does because of their initially higher rate.

The US became a great nation with none of our present income transfer schemes.

Collectivism

Collectivism is the participatory form of egalitarianism in which a group of people live and work together for a common purpose, equally sharing the necessary work and its rewards. This mode of social organization succeeds when all the participants believe in and are willing to subject themselves to a god and/or common purpose greater than themselves, and may join and leave at their own will. Trappist monasteries[1] and Israeli Kibbutzim[2] are good examples. So are families.

Applying this principle to a nation of millions of people with differing beliefs, motivations, and desires always leads to central control, unlimited government power, and the tyranny of those who claim to represent the supposed will of the people or the common good. It is inherently susceptible to corruption and capture by demagogues or even a true majority who believe themselves to embody the "people," as in Das Folk, the Proletariat, or the ninety-nine percent. It conjures images of masses of comrades marching in formation to a common beat.

Our republic properly sees government as a separate entity that performs certain limited functions, like delivering the mail or defending our borders, but that doesn't manage us.

Collectivism on a national scale is the ultimate denial of human uniqueness. It is purely utilitarian, with no regard for art or soul or passion. Its face is the anonymous apartment block and its veins are subway tubes.

Unlimited power is sometimes justified by the assertion that "Government is the name we give to the things we chose to do together."* It assumes society is one big religious order with common beliefs and intentions, and government exists to carry out a common purpose. An all-encompassing state subsumes everything and everyone in its sphere of influence.

There is an element of the collective state in most of the isms described here, but its fully-developed form appeared in Italian fascism in the early 20th Century. The dictator Benito Mussolini stated the principle in a speech in 1927.[3] "Everything in the State, nothing against the State, nothing outside the State"

The principles of collectivism are invoked to justify 51% of us forcing the other 49% to do something they would not choose to do. The state becomes a coercive force instead of a defender of liberty.

---

* This is often attributed to former Congressman Barney Frank, though I've been unable to locate the context. I believe he could have said it, but if he didn't, I apologize to him.

The problem is not that the majority imposes restrictive rules on a minority. Government properly does this all the time, as in declaring burglary a crime to be punished. The essence of legitimate restrictive rules is that a particular act is enjoined. The majority says "You may not do this." It does not force you to do something.

Collectivism is fundamentally different from government providing a service that its citizens may or may not choose to use, like libraries or parks. We democratically decide which public goods support our culture and are worth paying for, but we aren't required to use them, much less participate in them.

Taxes are a special case where we all must pay for the government to do specific things we explicitly authorize it to do. This puts a premium on requiring a large consensus on the major things government does, especially those that directly affect most people.

Progressivism

The American left once concentrated on better wages and working conditions for the laboring class, as exemplified by the AFL/CIO union movement.[4] The focus later shifted to rights for women and minorities, and later still to general improvements, or *progress*, in human behavior and life experience.[5]

The liberal tradition attempts to keep peace between people as they are, while progressivism attempts to improve people to what they should be. The progressive perspective is that the natural and good course of history is an arc of steady, if punctuated, progress toward a better society with adequate and mostly equal circumstances provided for all. Progressives wish to use government to encourage (read force) society in all its aspects to "progress" in this direction. Professor and later President Woodrow Wilson[6] was an early and eloquent advocate.

A pillar of progressivism is that most people can't be trusted to act in their own long-term interest. This may be the most fundamental difference between progressives and libertarians. Progressives seem to believe they are their brother's keeper. They want people not only to act in the interests of society, which is collectivism's ideal, but of their own. If this sounds extreme, consider that the federal government now chooses how citizens save for their old age and provide for their health care. It indirectly but strongly motivates them to make politically preferred choices about housing, energy, and charitable giving.

Liberty is depreciated except to the extent that it means freedom to live as one pleases, but with public support when the results are infelicitous, which enables irresponsible behavior. Medical care should be free, so we require motorcyclists to wear safety helmets to limit the public cost. More generally, no one should go without medical care, so we all must buy a standard insurance policy, even if some of us would rather make other arrangements for ourselves.

Progressives hold that the beliefs, ideals or principles that lead us to make improvident choices are wrong, so we must be directed to either change our beliefs or at least the actions that flow from them. Often, such as saving for old age or following a healthy regimen, their assessment is correct. The assault on liberty occurs when they force everyone to follow their prescription. They want to manage us as a rancher manages his cattle, which is a direct violation of the liberty rule that I won't try to force people to believe what I believe, even if they are wrong.

Interestingly, social control to improve people seems to work on small, local scales. David Brooks[7] of the New York Times points out that in impoverished places with poor social cohesion and often inadequate government, highly structured schools enforcing high standards can move young people from a road to failure onto a path to success. Attendance is voluntary, actually highly sought, and the teachers are dedicated to something beyond a salary and retirement. Unfortunately, these conditions cannot be replicated by government over a heterogeneous people.

Conservatives, and even more so libertarians, recognize and honor the natural differences in people and their desire to make their own distinct futures, so resist forceful measures to create a utopia. Progressives don't see this as an expression of an alternate policy and thus a legitimate form of opposition but rather as an inexplicable refusal to see the truth.

Need for Power

By having to force their ideas on people who aren't "ready" for them, progressives must necessarily gain government power. This makes for constant conflict with those who value liberty, or who just want the freedom to make their own mistakes. Resistance is seen as obstructionism or "chaos", preventing the government from "working." Attempts by opponents to correct prior overextension of government power and regain lost liberty are decried as a "Rollback of 50 years of progress," demonstrating a belief in the inevitability of the progressive agenda. The progressive concept of compromise is, therefore, at its most benign, to meet conservatives part way at each step of this journey, but always moving forward, that is, progressing.

History suggests that the progressive ideal can never be reached peacefully in a large diverse nation. My authorities are Benito Mussolini, cited above, and Karl Marx[8] who popularized the principle "From each according to his ability, to each according to his needs" in 1875. The subsequent Soviet Union tried to create a "New Soviet Man" [9] to realize this principle.

We know how that worked out.

A particularly evil instance of the idea of perfecting mankind was practiced in Nazi Germany[10] with echoes even in the United States.[11] Collectivist dictatorships have an absolute need to control the thoughts and beliefs of their subjects. Those who aren't sufficiently enthusiastic are exterminated[12, 13] or banished to re-education camps.[14]

Libertarians want neither to force people to make good choices nor indemnify them from the consequences of bad ones.

Application of the rules of liberty to government will go a long way toward correcting many of our social and political ills. As I see it, a better use for progressive energy would be to abandon their dreams of power, allow a significant reduction in central control, and shift to individually helping people adapt to the modern world without depending on the force of government. This would give us a more civil culture and might even encourage revival of local voluntary mutual aid societies that achieve some of progressivism's objectives without conflict or erosion of liberty.

The Sharing principle

Sharing as a primary virtue and a natural human attribute underlies several principles contrary to liberty.

The sharing principle is often expressed as a requirement for empathy toward the less fortunate. According to this view, we are not created materially equal as is incorrectly claimed we should be. Instead, we are who we are only partly by our own merit but for the most part as beneficiaries of the crapshoot of our genetic heritage and the efforts of the whole society. It is, therefore, our moral duty to have empathy and compassion toward others. Those of us lacking sufficient of these virtues must be forced to act by their strictures as directed by our moral superiors in government. This feeling can be encapsulated as

A primary purpose of government is to enforce a distribution (i.e. sharing) of material wealth entitling everyone to the amount required to satisfy his material needs.

The sharing principle is rarely stated so clearly. It is more often encountered as an unstated assumption in arguments such as "Liberty is fine in theory, but what about _____?" (Fill in the blank with something about someone hurting and needing help.) The unstated assumption is that the person needing help is entitled to it and the rest of us are obliged to share enough to make him or her well. An authentically compassionate person has jumped from the admirable emotion of wanting to help, to the authoritarian position of wanting to force others to be equally compassionate, thus canceling a moral position with an immoral one. Though signaling virtue, this approaches tyranny.

Doing something at the point of a gun (IRS enforcement) cannot be compassionate. Collecting taxes to furnish a public good is fundamentally different from collecting them just to turn around and give them to someone. Legitimate sharing, where one person shares with another, doesn't suffer this hazard because there is a direct connection between giver and receiver likely to benefit both in different ways. Reciprocal altruism and family duties bring the same benefits. Sharing via government is unidirectional anonymous forced transfers between strangers.

The sharing principle is justified by the benefits its embodiment provides to recipients, but the cost of things not done is never considered, and probably can't be because they don't happen. The people not hired because an employer keeps his headcount below some arbitrary number to avoid the costs of a social program are never charged against that program. Neither is the adult who accepts a modest life on disability because it's available, rather than seeking productive employment.

"Obamacare saved my life. Without it, I would be dead." [15] That program was certainly an immediate benefit to the speaker. But what was lost by the person forced to provide the money? What responsibility did the recipient have for prior measures to preserve her health, or that might even have degraded it? What had she done to care for herself before the need for medical intervention became acute?

Dependence

The sharing principle inevitably leads to dependence because being dependent is easier than being independent. Being a child is easier than being an adult. Being a pet is easier than being a wild animal. Over several generations, dependence can lead to surprising behavioral and even morphological changes.[16] The last thing we want is for our citizens to become genetically adapted to dependence.[17]

The sharing principle is not quite the same as egalitarianism. If productivity were high enough the basic needs of non-workers could be satisfied while leaving a surplus for the producers. Given enough increase in productivity from automation and artificial intelligence, we could have a society of a few well-compensated high producers, with an underclass of more-or-less comfortable people kept as pets.

Otherwise, the result is that everyone is simply equally poor. This is unlikely though because the people doing the distributing will always find ways to prosper.

The 1960 movie based on HG Wells' 1895 novella, *The Time Machine*, gives us a glimpse into such a world as experienced by the Eloi,[18] who ended up being food for their masters, and didn't even know it.

Fairness

Fairness is part of practically every political issue. Taxes[19] must be fair. Police procedures[20] must be fair. Housing[21] must be fair. Elections[22] must be fair. Everyone seems to want fairness. No one argues against it, so why is it such a constant issue? Is there perhaps confusion about what it means?

From the viewpoint of liberty, fair means impartial rules applying equally to all. That doesn't mean that the resulting lives will be equal, only that physical force will not be used to constrain them inequitably. Each person should be free to develop his or her own life as best he or she can without being forced to follow some other agenda or be subjected to arbitrary restrictions or demands. Fairness rejects social or cultural norms such as Jim Crow[23] when they are ultimately backed up by force.

In a family or other simple social context, fairness may mean equality in certain aspects, such as distribution of food or toys. Research shows that equality of possessions seems to be a natural desire of young children.[24] This meaning of fairness is reinforced when an adult seeing a child hoarding all the available toys naturally teaches them that such an unequal distribution is not "fair," which it isn't because it violates the reasonable familial rule of equality among the children. But the children simply learn that having unequal toys is unfair.

In this way, the meaning of *fair* is corrupted to support egalitarianism or other enforced conformity and is carried over into the much larger and more complex world of adult life.[25] This is the foundation of the fairness doctrine of John Rawls.[26] He's difficult to pin down to specifics but seems to suggest that government should enforce rules of property to provide everyone at birth with the same resources, including intelligence and environment, or compensation to make them effectively equal. Only then would different outcomes be "fair."

Equating fairness to equality and then trying to impose it by government force is doomed to fail because it denies reality.

The fact is *Life is not fair.* We are born with different abilities and deficiencies and in places with different natural resources, climates, and cultures. Accidents and luck happen.[27] Bad choices are made that cause future bad luck and accidents. Good luck is a confluence of preparation, awareness, and opportunity. In the modern world, preparation may take decades and the support of caring parents. Our task as independent conscious humans is to be aware of our situation and take whatever responsible actions are appropriate to make it the best we can.[28]

The best government can do is provide its citizens equal protection of the law. It must avoid or prevent the use of force to create unfairness. It should protect liberty.

Consequentialism

This is the principle that the government must do whatever is necessary to achieve whatever the holder feels is important. All that matters is the specific isolated intended result, or even the intention itself. It ignores niceties like constitutions or legislative process. Nothing should impede a policy having a desirable purpose. If the implementation of a policy does not achieve the desired ends, just expand the implementation. Or better yet, don't inquire too closely into the actual results. Focus on the intent. The ends justify the means, so don't look too closely at the means. Don't even look at the unintended or unseen consequences. Intent is everything.

The consequentialist is often emotionally invested in the cause of the moment and will not brook diversion by distinctions such as the constitutional difference between state and federal powers or having to wait for civil society to catch up with his or her passion. The cause must be satisfied, and now, not later. This probably describes most of the well-meaning citizens who just want life to be "right" for all without being distracted by formal principles, theories or ideals.

Mandatory minimum wages or employee benefits are perfect examples. Who could be opposed to people earning more, or receiving free health care? The beneficiaries are visible and usually grateful to the officials who enacted the laws that give them extra resources. The people not hired, or the businesses not started are not seen. The connection between the visible benefits and the spending power taken from those paying the bill is too obscure to be identified. The increase in the general cost of living is so diffuse that even though the nominal beneficiaries pay that along with everyone else, they are unaware of it. It just seems they have more money but aren't getting ahead.

Consequentialism inevitably erodes liberty and constitutional principles because of its laser focus on desires, whether they are couched as problems, needs, or justice. The political debate degenerates to nothing more than the merit of these desires. The costs in money or liberty come in a distant second in the public mind.

When combined with a tilt toward majority rule, this is fatal for liberty.

Pragmatism

Pragmatism is similar to consequentialism but sounds gentler and is frequently claimed as a virtue. A political argument may include the claim that the proponent is not ideological but rather, being a pragmatist, is above all that. The argument goes something like this.

- I only care about what works.
- The government must "solve" whatever "problem" the "private sector" doesn't.
- Many people don't make good decisions, so the government must decide for them.

The pragmatist is honestly unaware that the proposals following this argument usually come directly from principles contrary to liberty. These unexamined principles are held so deeply and fervently that they seem natural and should not be subject to philosophical attack or analysis. There can be no questioning for whom the proposal works, or at what cost in dollars, self-respect, or liberty. The pragmatist is the worst kind of idealist, one who doesn't even recognize or acknowledge his ideals. "Problems" are often abstractions recognizing that many people do not enjoy a full measure of happiness. *Private sector* is a belittling term for the civil society that is the actual creator of government, suggesting a naïve belief that the creation is wiser and more effective than the creator.

The pragmatist does not try to justify his policies on their own merit except as to a vague intent for nominal results. Critical thought is replaced by slogans such as "There is too much inequality." Valid statistical measures of inequality are claimed to justify income redistribution all by themselves without considering deeper principles. Whatever the pragmatist wants is good, and the only question is how to achieve it. His principles are clear from his policies to everyone but him. Many of those principles would be agreeable to Karl Marx.

It's also worth noting that the pragmatist may argue principles are poor guides to policy by judging them based on extreme extrapolation to ridiculous conclusions, such as equating liberty to license or some other distortion.

Moderation

Moderation[29] is just pragmatism with a willingness to admit there are competing principles, but the moderate is satisfied to compromise without reference to principle beyond "what is needed."

The *moderate* seeks to do what is "right" or what "works," without engaging in the difficult task of deriving principles that help decide what is not only a good result but a right process. A logical debate or argument is impossible when the participants cannot state, much less agree on, principles with which to evaluate legislative proposals. Without that, debate degenerates to a recitation of desires and unsupported anticipation of results.

There are moderate progressives and moderate conservatives, but they are different. The moderate conservative is willing to meet the progressive halfway toward some collectivist goal. The moderate progressive will do the same thing — that is, compromise halfway toward that same goal, accepting some delay in the progressive agenda, but seldom moving toward liberty.

Populism

Populism today seems to be an informal movement of people who feel, often with cause, that large impersonal forces such as governments or corporations unfairly prevent them from living an independent self-respecting life. They generally obey the rules of liberty in their own lives but are willing to bend them for defense against these mysterious forces. In this way, they partake of consequentialism, which suggests they can fall prey to unrealistic promises. In the past, American populism was an attribute of agrarian progressivism.[30] Those earlier farmers though had little in common with modern progressives.

Direct Democracy

We have a democratically based republic, not a direct democracy. The United States of America is neither the Unified State of America (unified, not united, and singular) nor the Peoples Republic of America. The United States of America was created as a union, not an amalgamation, originally of thirteen independent States. New states are admitted to the union as true States having their own distinct constitutions adopted by their citizens, not simply as regions or departments of a national State.

This federal system attempts a delicate balance between the values of deliberation and wisdom on one hand and a foundation of democratic consent of the governed on the other. Each has its strengths and risks. Deliberation and wisdom are necessary for good government but are subject to concentration of power, authoritarianism, and tyranny. Democracy has its merits but can degenerate to follow mass passions or selfish interests, ending with its own kind of tyranny. Maintaining liberty calls for a stable mix we are still seeking.

Nowhere has direct democracy resulted in a national government of any size or lasting prosperity, much less liberty.

Our federal structure is based on an early compromise that has served us well. Each state has two senators, but members of the House of Representatives are elected by districts having a nearly equal number of citizens, about 750,000. The Electoral College that formally chooses a president is a mixture in that each citizen has an equal vote in his or her state, and the number of electors from each state equals its House members plus two. But the states can direct all their electors to vote for the winner in that state. This offends pure democrats but works to preserve each state's identity in its federal representation. States must never be reduced simply to bureaucratic subdivisions managing federal programs.

Over the past century, we have expected and demand that the federal government satisfy more desires than it was ever designed to do. The consequence has been tension between our form of federal government and the uninformed idea that government should satisfy the desires of a democratic majority. The sad reality is that liberty must be defended from the very people charged with preserving it, namely us.

Technocracy and the Administrative State

This version of authoritarianism is the idea that the people are not smart enough or informed enough to make important decisions about their own lives, much less matters of state. Technocrats and their political masters have the hubris to believe they should make major decisions for the rest of us. This is kinder and gentler than the full-blown authoritarianism of Hitler, Mussolini, and Stalin, but the iron fist can be felt inside the velvet glove.

Ordinary citizens often express the principle as something like "If I were king for a day, I would [fill in the blank] to make this a better world." While usually intended as no more than a rhetorical flourish, such a statement reflects an acceptance of the notion that government should be responsible for organizing society and culture. One has only to listen to a panel of experts discussing how some program or market should function to discern the principle in action and sense their belief in their own superiority.

President Woodrow Wilson was an early proponent of supplanting constitutional government with one where real power lay with a trained professional bureaucracy organized as "a force of government agents absolutely free from the influence of politics." [31] But, of course, they would not be free from politics, only from the people.

The same tendency has crept into Congress and state legislatures. They both desire to regulate ever more aspects of our lives but are unwilling or unable to devote the time needed to consider the ramifications of their intentions, so they leave too much discretion to administrators, with the courts being complicit in this abdication of responsibility. [32, 33] With luck and better judicial appointments,[34] we may be able to reverse this trend.

The American progressive version of the administrative state isn't the only one that has been tried. It appears 2000 years ago in China as Confucianism,[35] which has formed an important part of East Asian public culture for centuries. Confucianism deserves respect for longevity, but liberty isn't one of its virtues. It's an early and continuing form of authoritarianism predicated on absolute monarchy or an equivalent form of permanent unitary political power directing a professional bureaucracy. The current Chinese leadership seems intent on obtaining the benefits of a market economy while retaining the total control required by the Confucian model. Good luck with that.

Unfortunately, it may be impossible to combine technocracy and liberty. Technocrats really do know more about their specialty than the rest of us, but they don't know our myriad priorities, prejudices, and circumstances. They are necessary for implementing policy but are toxic when charged with creating it. They cannot possibly know the countless market interactions that deliver local information too voluminous and varied in form to fit any humanly describable pattern or plan. Besides, their own preferences blind them to the diversity of those of the people. They become contemptuous of our inability to grasp the beauty and logic of their plans for us. The poster child for this feeling is Dr. Johnathon Gruber[36] who played a central role in designing Obamacare, and who was recorded stating that the public was too stupid to understand it and needed to be kept in the dark for it to pass Congress. This was not an aberration — it was the central thrust of the adoption and execution of the policy.

Liberal governance sets limits to prevent injury to others. It differs fundamentally from managing a purposeful system. In the former, the government says "Stop." In the latter, it tries to order us to go in a particular direction. It's the difference between traffic rules and the plan for a trip.

Conservatism

Conservatives' main principle for good government is respect for laws and institutions that have succeeded over time in providing prosperity and civil peace. They distrust proposals for sweeping changes in policy based on promises of large improvements in individual lives, especially when they depend on people acting collectively and more altruistically than they ever have. They are the main advocates for personal responsibility and freedom from coercion. In this way, they are a bulwark protecting liberty against encroachment by many of the contrary principles described here.

Conservatives support interpreting the Constitution in its original plain meaning only adapted as necessary to conform to modern usage, as in considering air traffic control to be in the same class as post roads and canals, or medicinal purity and safety to be on a par with weights and measures. They forcefully resist encroachment of the administrative state into our personal lives. Their philosophical home can be found in organizations such as the Heritage Foundation, the American Enterprise Institute and the Republican Party itself.

They depart from the principles of liberty by being willing to use government power to enforce what has long been regarded as good behavior but goes beyond liberty's simple strictures. For example, they are comfortable encouraging home ownership and churches by offering tax relief. They want to conserve a way of life they knew or imagined in the past. Opening public meetings and legislative sessions with prayers supports this feeling of community in their minds even though it discourages people holding different beliefs from joining them in political unity. They are comfortable using government power to discourage if not prevent people from harming themselves with drugs, alcohol or sexual promiscuity.

Some also consider sectarian religious prescriptions to be on a par with the liberties recognized by the Constitution. Examples would be the traditional understanding of marriage and various moral codes around personal relationships. The Constitution itself avoids such issues, which can go to the heart of liberty.

Identity Politics

Identity politics is a corruption of the natural tendency for people with common interests to band together for a stronger voice in the political arena. It lumps people into classes based on their genetics, country of origin, religion, sex, or age rather than on their character, ideas, or interests. It abandons the principles of liberty and individual identity for group "rights" or more accurately, entitlements. Citizens are reduced to ciphers in a grand accounting of group interests as defined by self-appointed spokesmen.

Identity politics is the tool of the demagogue and the racist. People are told they are victims cheated by others of their birthright. The demagogue promises to make them whole in return for their allegiance. They need not do anything difficult, just vote, and all will be well. The demagogue though will ensure that his clients always believe themselves victims, so they are perpetually in his thrall. Arranging for them to speak and think in their native language is one method. For example, federal rules require Medicare insurers to communicate with their clients in two dozen languages.[37] Gerrymandering them into real or virtual racial or ethnic ghettos[38] is tailor-made for the hustler who wants to be elected to public office.

Affirmative action rules and quotas stigmatize these clients so their difference is emphasized and perpetuated both for themselves and for the rest of the public, maintaining the need for special advocates — the demagogues. Assimilation into the general American culture puts the race hustler out of business.

The distinctions need not be racial or linguistic. The demagogue panders to people who are old, young, middle class, poor, or female — an endless supply of clients. They have only to be prevented from thinking of themselves as independent citizens.

Liberty is blind to these distinctions, at least for adults, and we expect government to be the same. The injury to liberty from unjust discrimination is not in recognizing and correcting the injustice but in endlessly exploiting its victims to gain power.

These arguments don't deny that people have burdens. We all do. They're just different.

Cosmopolitanism

The cosmopolitan or globalist pays greater allegiance to an idealized imaginary world community than to his or her own nation. Cosmopolitanism has elements of utopianism because it imagines an ideal world based on vague notions of perfection. These usually assume a substantial improvement in human nature and convergence to a single culture similar to but improved upon that of the advocate.

In advanced forms, this expanded allegiance can be to the earth itself, again in preference to a home identity. These transfers of allegiance are usually coupled with political adherence to principles of technocracy, egalitarianism, and progressivism. The danger here is these false premises can divert attention and international cooperation from real problems like global warming. Trying to cure this by a form of global government is likely to be worse than the disease because of the vast differences in principles of governance.

Woodrow Wilson was an early advocate, devoting major efforts of his presidency to creating, and urging the United States to join, the League of Nations.[39] He believed this assemblage of wise men could and should govern the world. (Yes, he meant men. He was very late in embracing the idea that women should participate in public affairs.)[40]

While the League of Nations was a failure, some agencies, such as the International Civil Aviation Organization (ICAO)[41], have succeeded as voluntary rule makers for cooperating countries and industries. This is not cosmopolitanism but simple cooperation among nations to provide safety in air travel, a classic public good.

Cosmopolitanism and its cousin multiculturalism are currently expressed partly as a rejection of the idea that there is anything exceptional about the United States. We are just one among many nations — no better and maybe a bit worse. We have no inherent right to control who or what enters our country or to limit our bounty to legal residents and citizens. While it may be argued that liberty demands such a hands-off approach to immigration and trade, world population and the illiberal cultures of many parts of the world suggest that liberty here could not survive control from abroad.

Multiculturalism

Multiculturalism[42] is the belief that all cultures are worthy of respect, an extension of brotherly love. It's an application of the liberty rule that "I won't try to force others to believe as I do."

At its best, multiculturalism is a celebration of distinct elements of other cultures that mirror liberty but in different dialects enriching the local culture in the process. At its worst, it tolerates principles hostile to liberty in the service of diversity. This happens when the culture in question accepts or encourages behavior that violates the rules of liberty or specific American laws.

Multiculturalism rejects the idea that America is a melting pot that melds people from many cultures into a common one of liberty, expressed by the motto *E Pluribus Unum* (Out of many, One.) Its preferred analogy is a salad bowl where the motto might be Semper Pluribus (Always Many), or Pluribus ad Infinitum (Many forever). If carried beyond appreciation of a rich and varied cultural heritage to maintenance of separate communities it leads to the evils of identity politics.

The uniqueness of American culture is its basis in liberty. This is the "pot" into which the cultures of immigrants should be "melted." Liberty says nothing about food, music, art, sports, or even social or family organization. It only forbids certain behavior. That is its virtue. Citizens can differ in all these and probably other aspects of culture with the confidence that if they follow the principles of liberty, they will be free to live their lives as they please. We don't have cultural police, only criminal police enforcing laws based on liberty.

Chapter 9

Religion

We owe ancient religions for some of the fundamental principles of liberty, and paradoxically also for some of the worst violations of liberty.

The oldest antecedents to the principles of liberty described in this book come from great thinkers in ancient China and Israel. For example,

"Don't do unto others what you don't want others to do unto you." Confucius[1] in the fifth century BC

"That which is despicable to you, do not do to your fellow, this is the whole Torah, and the rest is commentary, go and learn it." (*Babylonian Talmud*, Shabbat 31a), Rabbi Hillel[2] in the first century BC

These admonitions are similar to the Christian Golden Rule, "Whatsoever ye would that others should do to you, do ye even so to them." *King James Bible*, quote from 30 AD[3] — But note the subtle difference. The Christian rule requires its adherents to actively do something while the others simply require restraint. All allow some discretion in that they depend on what one would wish done or not done to oneself, but the earlier rules seem more circumscribed even to the point of being reasonably well defined. The Golden Rule includes anything that one might want another to do, which is unlimited.

The modern concept of liberty as it relates to the right to hold beliefs independently of authority appears with European Christian thinkers mostly concerned with direct access to biblical ideas without having to depend on the intermediation of the Roman Church. The resulting protestant faiths fostered much of the individualism and market freedom underlying the founding of the United States of America.[4]

We owe a great debt to these early thinkers. Their ideas were probably not common in their times, or they wouldn't have felt the necessity to state them as rules or challenges to authority. For that matter, their principles are far from universally practiced today, which is why the idea of liberty has to be sold and, while widely but not universally accepted, needs defense by a strong government.

All religions accumulate volumes of additional strictures regulating many and in some cases all aspects of life. Liberty is diminished when the adherents of a sect transform these accretions into secular law. Recall that one of the rules of liberty requires that "I don't try to force (others) to believe what I believe even if I'm convinced they're wrong." and I don't allow my government to do that either. This rule may be the hardest to observe.

How much a government allows freedom of religion is a good measure of its commitment to liberty in general. United States governments at all levels scrupulously avoid any suggestion of favoring one religion over another or none at all.

Problems of public safety and national security arise though because our governments are uncomfortable defining what kind of organization or activity qualifies as a religion. We are also uncertain about what kind of speech or assembly constitutes preparation for or the actual conduct of treason.

The other way religions can potentially be a problem for liberty is that many of their precepts come literally from insights about the physical world and society held by wise men of their formative eras. They did the best anyone could with the knowledge available at the time, but that was limited to what could be discovered with none of the technical and intellectual tools developed in the past few centuries, especially in the past hundred years. They had no conception of the vastness of the universe in time and space both great and small. They knew nothing of the evolution of the universe or of life itself. An authoritarian culture was usually necessary for survival. Finally, it could hardly occur to them that humans might one day fill the earth to its capacity to support them.

The danger religion poses to liberty is that the followers of these wise teachers have often taken the reports of their insights as literal commands from a transcendent perfect being and not susceptible to improvement by human intelligence. Subsequent interpretation by fallible men has often caused immense grief.

We can profitably respect these ancient traditions for what they teach us about getting along with each other and for reminding us there is more to the world or the universe then we know. But we can be selective and critical about adopting them wholesale.

Chapter 10

Liberty and Tough Issues

The principles of liberty can guide us when hard problems are dropped at the door of government.

Civil Rights

Obligations on Government

I remember as I entered college in 1955 hearing of Rosa Parks' arrest[1] in Montgomery, Alabama for not yielding her bus seat to a white passenger, as required of black people by state law. That seemed wrong then and still does. As a graduate student in 1961, it also seemed wrong that Negroes (now African Americans) were refused service at a lunch counter. These feelings arose without the benefit of clear concepts of liberty or civil rights. What happened was just wrong. Maturity and analysis have refined my understanding.

The rules of liberty are inherently non-discriminatory. The basic rule that "I don't hit people unless they physically attack me" doesn't put qualifications on *people*. Use of force in these situations clearly violates liberty.

But beyond the use of force, government has an additional responsibility to treat all citizens equally in all its functions, for example, voting, because there is only one government (at each level) and it belongs to all of us. We as citizens are at liberty to respect and associate freely with anyone but are not required to do so. Government is — and it must do so equally without favor or prejudice.

The aspirations of liberty proclaimed at our founding were not universally observed at that time. Some aspects of liberty have been so contentious that statutes, constitutional amendments, and even war have been necessary to achieve them. Our first and longest conflict following independence (and the war of 1812) was opposition to official racial discrimination starting with the Civil War and emancipating the slaves, continuing through Reconstruction, the 14th Amendment, integration of the military by President Truman, and culminating in the Civil Rights Act of 1964[2] and the Voting Rights Act of 1965[3]. Almost equally contentious was women's suffrage, settled nationally by the 19th Amendment[4] in 1920.

A few isolated issues such as equal access by women to the Marine Corps[5] combat infantry remain, but the central issue of government discrimination by race, sex, and other factors has in the main been resolved. We are left with the question of the degree to which government power should enforce a similar level of even-handedness, or civility, on individuals.

Civility includes qualities such as respect, tolerance, kindness, politeness, acknowledgment, acceptance, forbearance, hospitality, inclusiveness, warmth, and grace, which are admirable when sincerely expressed. These go far beyond the demands of liberty, which proscribe only physically harmful behavior, to describing positively good, or civil, behavior usually having only an incidental physical element, if any.

As a general social policy, being civil to each other is a good idea, but what does that mean and how much force is appropriate to attain it? There is nothing, though, in the rules of liberty that requires one person to like another. "I don't try to force them to believe what I believe even if I'm convinced they're wrong" means I won't try to force one person to like another or even be polite.

How should this apply to people serving the public as a business?

Obligations on Business

Strict application of liberty would not require anyone to do anything, such as serving a sandwich to a person to whom the server has a personal animosity. Failing to act cannot be a crime under the rules of liberty, though it may be a breach of contract or of a responsibility that one assumes voluntarily. For example, a doctor or a police officer has a duty to act in certain circumstances. The Civil Rights Act broke new ground by effectively regarding businesses open to the public as having assumed a responsibility to serve everyone. It also tacitly assumed that all businesses are engaged in interstate commerce, which the federal government has constitutional authority to regulate. Thus we have the principle that service cannot be refused simply based on race, which has been generalized to include other personal characteristics including sex, religion, disability and unusual gender situations.

This demand is justifiable because requiring a business to provide its ordinary service to all is much less of a burden than that on a customer denied service simply because of his race. Even though this creeps into the realm of requiring specific acts by individuals, namely associating with someone they might not respect, it makes sense because a business leaves some of the liberty due an individual behind when it opens its doors to the public and depends on public licensing and services to prosper. Thus, law evolves.

Requiring individuals operating as a business, as opposed to the State, to treat people equally is a significant addition to our constitutional principles, which grant the federal government no power to improve culture or enforce civility. Enforcing tolerance on individuals is significant and we must consider its ramifications and necessary limitations, and not carry it too far. Individuals have feelings and beliefs, unlike government. Enforcing civility tests the boundaries between mores and law even at the state level. We should not venture beyond tolerance to acceptance and endorsement; from rights to entitlements; from passive acceptance to active participation. We are trying to balance freedom against coercion while avoiding the tar pit of thought control.

Government is well suited for punishing crimes such as murder, robbery, and fraud. However, it's less successful at causing positive acts of good behavior. This may be because there is consensus on what constitutes criminally bad behavior, but much less on which good behaviors should be enforced by law, which means police with guns.

Churches are better at this, perhaps because we don't give them police powers. They must rely on persuasion. (This may be the main objection to fundamentalist religions having secular power. They try to do both, with grotesque results in conflict with liberty).

But legal evolution doesn't stop when a principle is codified. Real cases illuminate uncertainties in meaning. Are there prudent limits to requiring individuals acting as businesses to treat all customers equally, and what does that mean?

Public Accommodation

The consensus now is clear, and I believe widely held, that to refuse service to a person based only on characteristics of birth or beliefs is wrong and should be illegal.

In the early civil rights cases, the vendor was wrong in refusing to provide something normally for sale simply because of the potential buyer's skin color. The restaurant was not being asked to provide something not on the menu. We don't require restaurants to provide kosher meals, but they may do that as a way of enhancing their business. A fine restaurant may require its male guests to wear a coat and tie but cannot require them to be white. It may offer a vegetarian meal but cannot be required to do so.

Now we come to wedding cakes, and how they differ from ham sandwiches.

The question is how far government should go along the spectrum from preventing actual harm to individuals, to "correcting" the social conventions that underlie discriminatory acts or thoughts. An important principle of governing in support of liberty is to consider government as something established by the people of a culture to serve that culture, not an instrument to mold the culture. Above all, government should do no harm. Recent court cases[6] have it doing more harm than good.

On one side of the issue, a small but growing number of citizens are developing an understanding that the close bonds associated with couples in a traditional marriage should be available to and recognized for couples of the same sex. This is consistent with liberty. There are questions as to exactly how these bonds should be recognized in law, but the principle is clear and unobjectionable.

At the same time, there are citizens who find same-sex marriage, however it's defined, to be unacceptable on moral or theological grounds. And a very small number of these citizens own and operate bakeries that create and sell wedding cakes of a conventional nature, some decorated with expressions of felicitation such as "Congratulations on your Wedding," or "Good Luck Alice and Bob." Some may be topped by figures of a (male) groom and (female) bride.

Dilemma

Now imagine two men walk into the bakery. They wish to buy a cake topped by two men in tuxedos, decorated with "Good Luck George and Roger." The baker says he'll sell them a generic wedding cake, but he won't decorate one as they request because doing so would violate his beliefs. He is being asked to create a thing he has never created or sold, and which would be deeply offensive to him. What can liberty tell us about the equities here?

The first avenue is to seek an agreeable compromise. The baker might offer to sell the men a cake saying "Congratulations on your Wedding" because that is a standard item for him, and he might even offer to sell them a pair of tuxedo-clad male figures they could affix to the cake as they wish because these figures are also standard items. Even though he knows the situation and doesn't like it, he would not be performing an actual act against his moral principles. The men might accept this as a generous accommodation of their unusual circumstance. Or they might not. In that case, their remedy is to go down the street to another baker who doesn't give a fig who marries whom and is glad to have the business.

But what if the men are adamant and insist on forcing this particular baker to act as though he believes as they do about marriage? Using the force of law to attain this result would clearly violate one of the rules of liberty.

Consider the question as one of equity. Which is the greater harm, forcing the baker to violate a core belief, or requiring the men to seek another vendor for a decoration for their wedding? I think it's fair to assume that such a vendor can likely be found because the baker does not have a monopoly. He has not refused to serve these men because of any characteristic of theirs, he has only declined to create something that he has never done, and for a strong personal reason. We can object if the baker refuses to sell them a standard cake solely because of their beliefs, but not if he declines to actively participate in their ritual.

This situation differs fundamentally from a lunch counter refusing to serve an African American a ham sandwich. That was a standard item on its menu, and the refusal was based solely on the customer's skin color. That kind of discrimination has properly been determined to violate public policy.

Resolution

But you might say "They just wanted a cake." No, they wanted the baker to create a thing that expressed a belief he felt was wrong. One can seldom know another's inner motivations, but it's also possible that creating public acceptance of a novel meaning of marriage might have been the motivation for the request, with the cake only a means. In any case, application of the rules of liberty has allowed us to clarify and resolve a difficult issue. The general conclusion can be stated as "Public policy demands that all vendors open to the public offer their standard products to anyone regardless of their identity, but no more."

Providers of unique services such as artists, architects, or dress designers would seem immune to such a request because their service is so personal that a potential client knowing that the artist opposed some aspect of the client would realize that the final product could not be the artist's best because of that very fact. The only plausible reason to force an artist into such an arrangement would be to force an expression of belief that the artist did not hold, and so would violate the principle of liberty discussed here.

As a final note, it is important to base the argument on beliefs rather than religion. This issue at its core is about freedom of belief in general, not the practice of religion.

Abortion

Abortion is one of the most intense, divisive and least tractable issues that has faced the United States for the past half-century because it directly affects half the population (women) in a way intimately connected with their bodies and life itself. And most of the other half feels just as strongly. The crux of the matter is the extent to which abortion should be prohibited by law, invoking the police power.

Beyond the question of rights, abortion is a profound failure of responsibility. The mother and father by conceiving a child have taken on the responsibility for raising it. This implies a commitment of some twenty years of their lives. The father may fail simply by disappearing. The mother must make a more difficult personal decision. She too, though, may fail in her responsibility. The result is a tragedy.

What should be the public policy response in the form of law?

Conflict of Rights

Clearly, the baby's right to life is violated with extreme prejudice. Rights don't get more fundamental or more elusive to delineate in time than that. Should the State then force the mother to carry the baby to term? This would violate her right to ownership of her own body, another fundamental principle of liberty. She would be but a vessel. Laws on the subject target the person performing the procedure rather than the woman, but ultimately, she is responsible and must be the primary subject of policy.

There can be no compromise or middle ground between these principles. Moderation is not a viable path. Can any of the other principles for public policy shine a beacon to guide us past the rocks upon which our ship of state would founder by following either of these two principles alone?

A collectivist approach might be to relieve the parents of responsibility by claiming that society through the agency of government is responsible.[7] The implications here are terrible. First, the government would need to control the original conception. Then the government would need to take custody of the mother during her pregnancy and ultimate delivery. No, let's leave the responsibility with the parents.

We can step back and ask whether this issue is better resolved by civil society or by law. One principle for the design of government is we don't want it to take on responsibilities for which it is ill-equipped. Attempting to settle an unresolvable conflict between equal rights seems to be a perfect example of such an impossible problem. The most government can do about personal behavior is punish it or pay for it, and neither is appealing here.

No Government Resolution

The logical conclusion is that government should decline to be involved. The states should not exercise their police power in prohibiting it, and neither they nor the federal government should pay for it. Because abortion is a matter of civil rights, albeit of a special kind, Congress should enact appropriate prohibitions, or failing that, the Supreme Court could issue an appropriate ruling on constitutional grounds. Abortion should be removed from the realm of law.

Admitting that the problem is too hard and there should be no law on the subject one way or the other is anathema to partisans and ideologues, but it's true, at least for a government based on liberty.

Not that letting the State off the hook means society endorses abortion — far from it. We have to accept that for some or even many issues the government should take no position. The organs of civil society (churches, volunteer groups, scholars, even sidewalk protesters) should be free to argue their cases to the fullest extent, but not to use the power of the State or any other kind of physical force to prevail. An open debate without rancor and with support toward the humanity and anguish of the mothers might be more effective and healthier for society than what we have now. It will also have the virtue of putting the argument on a higher plane than one of coercion.

The idea that government may leave itself out of an issue is profoundly conservative but may be regarded as radical because it contradicts the last century of American political history.

But note that for this issue the results of government involvement have not been agreeable. We, both common citizens and deep thinkers, have struggled with this for close to a century without resolution and with a nearly equal split of judgment. It's just too hard, so don't risk losing respect for the law by trying to solve it by law.

Hate Crime

The federal government has recently created a new class of criminal offense called *Hate Crime*. This crime is distinct from the common law crimes of murder, assault, and arson normally tried by state courts. The essential element of the crime is the state of mind of the perpetrator. Besides the usual requirements that the accused intended to do the act and knew it is wrong, to be convicted of a hate crime the accused must be found to have had a particular animus against the victim based on race or some other special quality. In effect, the hate crime statute criminalizes a thought or belief that is followed by an act that is also a crime in itself.

This seems wrong on several grounds. First, the rules of liberty deny me the right to force anyone to believe what I believe or to not believe something with which I disagree. Second, it is unnecessary because a state judge in sentencing under normal criminal statutes can consider such factors in deciding the severity of punishment. Third, creating a new and separate federal crime subjects an accused to double jeopardy when he has been found not guilty of the primary crime in state court.

Hate Speech

So far, the United States has not defined the crime of hate speech, but Canada[8,9] and other countries have. [10,11] American universities are committed to suppressing what they call hate speech. [12,13] So what exactly is hate speech and to what extent should it be suppressed?

Definitions are fluid, but common elements cover a range from causing distress to being likely to result in discrimination or violence. They always depend on a presumed effect induced in another, unidentified, person. There need not be an actual victim required to give evidence and be subject to cross-examination at trial. No proof of damage is required.

Such laws are a gross violation of free speech and are unnecessary to boot. We already have laws against defamation, libel, and conspiracy to commit crimes. We must not erode our liberties to prevent hurt feelings.

Free Speech

We are guaranteed freedom of speech by the rules of liberty and the US Constitution. Government may not punish us for the content of our speech outside of some very narrow restrictions on libel and conspiracy. Any opinion on a public issue is protected.[14] Americans forget how unusual, possibly unique, this is in the world. Quite a few colleges have official polices restricting free speech, though the number is falling.[15,16,17] Even some professors at otherwise respectable universities depreciate free speech in their efforts to suppress opinions with which they disagree.[18,19,20]

Freedom to speak does not, though, include the right to speak in such a way that it prevents another person from speaking, as for example making so much noise or disruptive violence at a forum that the intended speaker is prevented from proceeding. Nor does it oblige anyone to listen, or confer an entitlement to a venue or an amplifier. It doesn't even assure equal time at a public forum. It most assuredly doesn't include a right to riot even if some rioters carry signs with political messages. It doesn't confer a right to disturb the peace at an official's home by shouting amplified speech opposing his policy.

These corruptions of the right to free speech are examples of a dangerous trend toward failure to use language with even a modicum of care much less precision. Defense of liberty requires that riot, vandalism, and disturbing the peace be prosecuted for what they are, crimes pure and simple. Too often they are excused because of a misguided deference to the right of free speech or assembly.

Being free to speak means no government can jail us for the content of our speech, period. But that's a lot.

War

It's paradoxical and contradictory to some, but the object of war in a nation dedicated to liberty is to keep the peace. Peace is the absence of coercion, not the absence of war. Hungary's Lajos Kossuth put it plainly in the 19th century, "I hope I shall never mistake oppression for peace." In a dictatorship, absolute monarchy, or theocracy there may be no visible violence and it may be safe to walk the streets without fear of attack, but the lack of freedom to choose is far from a state of peace. South Korea, where a city of ten million is within range of massive batteries of hostile artillery, is not at peace.

Simply stating that we, as a nation, are not at war, or that war is obsolete, does not make it so. Protestations of peace do not stop an invading army or falling missile. When tanks roll across the border, missiles re-enter the atmosphere, or a pirated airliner hits an office building is too late. Liberty recognizes the right and necessity of self-defense. The only issue is determining when the conditions are appropriate and what means to use.

Hard and fast rules are elusive, though it might be worthwhile to codify the circumstances in which nuclear weapons can be employed at the initiation of conflict. We must by constitutional means choose and trust prudent, wise, and skilled leaders for this and give them the tools and support to do the job. There is no easy way or formula around this problem. That's the best we can do.

Global Warming

Protecting the livability of our environment from a warming global climate should be as legitimate a federal responsibility as any national-scale hazard. And that legitimacy suffers from the same lack of constitutional authority as environmental control in general. We need a full and rational debate on the nature and extent of the problem followed by drafting an appropriate constitutional amendment granting the federal government necessary powers to enact laws and make treaties. The Constitution has been amended for less critical issues, and there is no reason to proceed without doing it again. Attempting to enforce laws, taxes, and regulations without proper authority is a formula for government gridlock at best and tyranny at worst. We have a preview of this in recent attempts to commit the United States to major taxes and restrictions on commerce via adoption of a treaty with neither constitutional authority nor congressional approval.[21]

The issue is difficult to resolve because proposed solutions have outpaced firm scientific understanding of the myriad complex factors that drive warming, and public understanding is even less. The issue has become mired in partisan rhetoric with positions firming emotionally in the absence of knowledge and presence of overblown forecasts of catastrophe. Deeply held convictions or wishful dreaming about desirable directions for societal evolution conjure visions of either a simpler life using less energy or magical sources of energy that carry no risk. Such dreams usually also involve an increase in regimentation.

Dire warnings about global warming also carry an element of moral superiority relative to those counseling caution in forcing major changes to our economy based on imperfect knowledge. The latter are accused of denying the truths of "science" [22] while the believers in central control and particular solutions claim not only to be realists but better people.[23]

A book on liberty is not the place for this debate. It is, though, appropriate to point out that part of the difficulty in considering and resolving this issue is that the federal government has become bogged down in matters not truly national in nature and scope, preventing it and the public from devoting time and energy to actual national issues like this one.

Gay (and Other) Marriage

Gay marriage has arisen as a public policy issue because the logic of liberty conflicts with age-old tradition and because the institution of marriage has accrued layers of governmental restrictions and benefits.

Our laws never had to define marriage because everyone understood what it meant. New understandings of intimate long-term relationships require us to develop appropriate laws for corresponding rights, entitlements, and obligations. It seems to me that the way to resolve the conflict is to separate the various parts, and then reconstruct something that satisfies both the new understandings and the principles of liberty.

My approach is to remove government from the business of defining marriage, at least as far as the concept depends on religious or cultural tradition. Government is not very good at this because it implies either a widely held consensus, which is obviously not present—or significant coercion. If the issue is one of personal morals or belief, government should not be involved. What government is good at, though, is enforcing contracts and protecting the weak. For government to enforce a contract its courts must be able to determine what was contracted. That is, to what did the parties intend to agree? This is always best done by reference to a written document.

Written Contracts

I envision an evolution of several kinds of more or less standard agreements, much like real estate purchase contracts, that describe different living arrangements. People who want to live in a committed relationship would be free to choose which one suited them or write their own, execute it appropriately, and go on with their lives together. They could call their relationship whatever they wished and could sanctify it in the religious or cultural tradition of their choice. In fact, many modern marriages do something of this nature by writing their own vows, or by executing formal prenuptial agreements.

The government would not be naming or defining these relationships; it would only be there to enforce the written agreements as appropriate.

Existing laws relating to marriage should be amended to reflect standard elements of these agreements. That is, if the parties agree to merge their finances, then the government could extend appropriate tax advantages if that is the consensus of public policy. Similarly, if the parties agree that one partner expects to earn the bulk of income while the other keeps house and nurtures children, then our present property division rules incident on divorce may be appropriate. As with any contract, these could be amended if both parties agree.

As to protection of the weak, the obvious major issue is children. We seem to be moving toward a legal doctrine that protects children as individuals anyway, so that should not be a serious problem. Couples who conceive and bear or adopt children would by that fact put themselves in the role of parent, with all that implies legally, just as now. If government needs to protect adoptees, the responsible agency could refer to the existing agreement between the requesting adopters as part of its evaluation of their suitability.

Similarly, rules regulating marriage or cohabitation of minors would be expressed in terms of the enforceability of these contracts and could carry the same restrictions and sanctions as presently.

Besides removing heat from the current issue, this approach should also have a substantial secondary benefit. At present, starry-eyed couples can marry without giving much thought to the long-term implications. If they had to select, read, agree to and sign a formal contract laying out their responsibilities, they might be more circumspect.

Firearms

Another issue that cleaves the American public down the middle is possession and "bearing" of firearms. Shelves full of learned and not-so-learned volumes have been written parsing the right to keep and bear arms. Recalling that the Constitution recognizes but does not create or grant rights, we can avoid the thorn bush of dissecting the Second Amendment and base our argument on liberty.

I don't hit people unless they physically attack me. Then I do, and I do it as effectively as necessary and possible under the circumstances.

Self Defense

This is not the place to refine the meaning of *attack, effectively, necessary,* or *circumstances,* but the right would seem to apply to a peaceful citizen set upon by one or more thieves either in public or at home. In the brief seconds of an unexpected attack, social policy and the attacker's life history are irrelevant. We don't need to examine the relative wisdom of self-defense vs. acquiescing in the attacker's demands. At that moment, the decision to defend belongs only to the victim. The attackers have put themselves in mortal danger by their threats or acts and have no legitimate complaint about the results.

Reason and prudence apply here as in other issues of law. A private citizen, as opposed to a trained police officer or professional bodyguard, should be expected to react in a less predictable manner, possibly with more force than upon reflection might have been necessary. Prudence demands that such a person, that is most of us, be approached with courtesy rather than aggressively. It also demands that no one be threatened with a realistic appearing toy gun. Stupid can be fatal.

Reason also suggests we are unlikely to be surprised by a military attack. Weapons such as armor in the hands of malefactors should be detectable by our government before they can be put to much use. We don't individually need crew-served anti-tank weapons. We can debate the individual need for automatic weapons.

Using personal weapons to defend against tyranny in the United States of America seems inappropriate and unnecessary. The value of the peace preserved by accepting our judicial system outweighs any injustice that system has imposed. We possess adequate means to protect liberty against government usurpation of power so long as we exercise them by informed voting. Restricting government to its legitimate functions will go a long way to reducing the conflicts that cause some to consider armed rebellion. Anyone who believes he needs recourse to arms to defend against our government would do well to consider that he might possibly be mistaken.

Diversity

Liberty celebrates diversity. We don't think alike and don't want the government trying to make us do so. Some of us will be more comfortable calling 911 and waiting for the police to arrive than others. Some will feel better by providing their own emergency protection. Within the rules of liberty (*I don't try to force them to believe what I believe even if I'm convinced they're wrong.*) we don't assume we can speak or decide for them. We must make every reasonable attempt to accommodate different ways of regarding the world.

Firearms are deadly weapons. That's what they're for. They are also reasonably considered by many citizens to be necessary tools for self-defense, as well as for recreational and rural occupational purposes. A governmental role in accommodating these diverse applications while recognizing the danger is clearly appropriate. The question is how.

Politics

The issue has been corrupted by those who would deny all firearms to private citizens through an incremental approach imposing a seemingly infinite progression of increasing restrictions. The understandable reaction of many exercising the right to be armed has been to dig in our heels and resist regulations that while reasonable in their title (e.g. "background checks") are potentially more intrusive than necessary to protect public safety. We have a cycle of unreal assumptions, unjust restrictions, and ineffective discourse. We are stuck arguing absolutist positions which violate some principle of liberty.

The first step is to recognize this is not a federal issue, except in the special case of interstate commerce (that is actually commerce.) States are responsible for public safety within broad restrictions protecting liberty as expressed in the Second Amendment. They need not take a common approach, though nothing is wrong with states reconciling their firearms laws as they do driving rules, which are similar but not identical. Large states could even have different rules for different counties if the affected citizens want them and the state can enforce them.

The interest groups need to get together and agree citizens have the right to defend themselves by means of firearms. They also need to agree there is an inherent risk from such uses, and reasonable standards for recognizing responsible uses, users, and weapons must be established. Once these ground rules are settled, reasonable legislators and judges[24] should be able to craft rules that allow most citizens to keep and bear most types of small arms at home and in most public places.

Health Care

Political Issue

Health care has become a dominant political issue because it affects everyone in critical matters of life, can be a large, unpredictable, sometimes devastating personal expense, and has become a major cost for employers and governments. The emotional impact leads to calls for government to "do something" to make the pain go away.

The industry represents almost one fifth[25] (18 %) of the US gross domestic product, which implies that it employs a similar fraction of the working population. The annual cost works out to roughly $10,000 per person. These magnitudes alone make it important.

Federal and state governments have responded by enacting laws (Medicaid, Medicare, and Obamacare[*])[26] that attempt to share these costs collectively in what may be the largest income transfer scheme in history. Much of the cost has been hidden, first by massive borrowing that has expanded the national debt to historic and probably unpayable levels, and second by forcing people to buy mischaracterized "insurance" they don't believe they need at inflated prices to subsidize others.

The importance of health care to everyone throughout the country makes it a nationwide issue, but the nature of medical care is local and personal, not national. Federal overreach has exacerbated the problem. Can we do better? Let's examine the parts.

---

[*] The Patient Protection and Affordable Care Act of 2010

Health Care a Right?

In most discussions of health care policy, the unmentioned elephant in the room is personal responsibility. Many people simply want someone else to be responsible for their health, like when they were children. It's comforting to believe that a benevolent government will deliver us from pain and suffering. This feeling and the universal need for medical care at some point in our lives leads to the assertion that such care is a right. For example, a group called, "Health Care for All Oregon", asserts that universal government-paid medical care is a right.[27] As discussed earlier, this misunderstands, or purposefully misuses, the concept of a right, as well as confusing health with medical care. The argument for medical care as an entitlement, not a right, is rarely heard because then any program would have to be justified as such, including identifying who bears the corresponding obligation and the nature of that obligation.

Responsibility

Each adult is ultimately responsible for his own health and welfare because each of us is the nexus of beliefs, motivations, practices, interventions, consequences, and benefits that constitute the arena of our health condition. No one else, and certainly not a legislator or bureaucracy, can know or care about these as we do ourselves. When faced with a health care issue, it may be appealing to mentally transfer this responsibility to a doctor, a hospital, or even government. But responsibility means to bear the consequences of failure. It's not simply to be in charge or pay for something. While sympathetic and acting fiducially, the doctor will not live with our condition and therefore does not have the same responsibility as ourselves, and the others have less. Furthermore, government resources are not a genie coming out of a magic lamp, but the property of some other actual person. We must conclude that although we may try to shift our responsibility, we can't.

On a practical level, a major health factor is one's lifestyle, especially regarding diet, exercise, and avoidance of unhealthy substances. No one else can be fully aware of our habits, much less control them for us. Forcing others to accept our risk without the corresponding control would be a major violation of their liberty, as would be a loss of that control to ours. Entering into an arrangement where we give over our responsibility would leave us no better than cattle, where their owner is responsible for their health and welfare until he sells them. Being forced into such an arrangement would be especially onerous. If we give government the responsibility for our health, it logically needs the power to manage the factors affecting that health, not just medical care. It would shift from governing us to managing us. Major decisions would be made by officials to design and apportion medical services according to political priorities.

The motorcycle helmet law is an example of this logic in action. Because much medical expense is currently a public cost, we logically require riders to take precautions to reduce their risk. There is no reason this logic could not be extended to require us to join exercise classes and eat broccoli.

An individual's hospital stay is a personal, consumable non-public good that is not a legitimate application of the general welfare concept. Under the rules of liberty, no one is entitled to someone else's property for his own use. Wishing for or asserting that does not make it so. Medical care is a part of our personal responsibility, neither a right nor an entitlement. People who take care of their own health shouldn't be required to pay extra for those who don't.

We can, of course, join with others in voluntary associations of many kinds such as extended families, mutual aid societies, or as policyholders with insurance companies to spread the cost of risk, but these choices are ours and ours alone. They alter the form but not the substance of our responsibility. One way or another we are responsible for our own health.

The Health Care Market

Mischaracterizing health care as a right is equivalent to asserting that it should not be considered a market service, but as a cost-free good available for the taking, like freedom of speech. According to this view, no one should need to think of cost in the way deciding to buy anything else is considered. But medical care is not cost-free. The doctors, nurses, and support staff who provide it must be paid. Expensive buildings, equipment, and supplies must be purchased.

Understanding markets tells us that one as large and complex as our healthcare industry and all its clients, which together are the market, is far beyond the capacity of any central authority to understand, plan or manage. The complexity of and rancor around legislation is proof.

A speculative but plausible argument is that infusion of vast amounts of federal money into a market where most buyers pay little or nothing for each transaction is bound to increase prices. In contrast, when medical services are provided in an unsubsidized market, costs decline while quality improves. This has been demonstrated for cosmetic surgery [28] and medical tourism.[29] It's likely that past attempts to insulate people from medical costs have had the perverse consequence of increasing those very costs.

We may accept the principle of personal responsibility and the conclusion that federal attempts to provide or mandate individual health care cannot succeed, but it is still true that medical care is expensive and is needed at somewhat unpredictable times. What can and should government do to alleviate this?

Experience tells us to look for prior government actions or market conventions that have exacerbated the problem. Eliminating such causes is better than covering up their bad effects with new laws. A market-based economy not only

202

supports liberty but has led to what is arguably the highest standard of living in history, at least for those who fully participate in it. So, let's see where our healthcare market has been distorted and restrained so as to lose some of this benefit and make some cautious suggestions about how it can be improved.

Insurance

Before we think about insurance, we need to correct a conceptual error that has bedeviled rational analysis. Almost the entire national discourse on financing medical care is based on falsely calling it insurance. Virtually every public program in this area is actually cost-sharing of prepaid full-spectrum medical care. This is more than a pedantic issue of semantics. It prevents productive thinking.

The concept of insurance has earned wide public acceptance based on the industry's history of spreading the risk of expensive unforeseen events over large numbers of people who willingly pay modest premiums to avoid a devastating unexpected cost. The advocates of government supported health care like to call it insurance to steal some of that public acceptance, but this is dishonest. If they mean socialized or subsidized medicine, they should call it that. The present programs have almost nothing in common with insurance.

No insurance covers the cost of painting a house or replacing a worn-out roof, and certainly not mowing the lawn or washing the dishes. We know we are responsible for this routine maintenance and if we don't do it, we will probably have much larger costs eventually. There is no point in trying to transfer the responsibility to someone else.

Insurance is based on infrequent and unexpected loss like car crashes or fires, unlike routine costs of maintaining good health.

Advocates may assert that health insurance should cover routine doctor visits because without full coverage people are less likely to seek care for initial symptoms that, if diagnosed and treated early, may avoid more serious and expensive treatment later. This argument denies the responsibility that everyone has for maintaining his own health. It exemplifies the progressive inclination to regard the general citizenry as not up to managing their own lives.

Underwriting

Underwriting, the art and science of estimating the likelihood that an identifiable class of policyholders will experience a certain amount of loss in a certain period, is an essential element of insurance. For example, young single men driving powerful sports cars pay a larger auto insurance premium than middle-aged family men driving sedans because experience shows the former have more or larger claims. Life insurance, which pays a fixed amount upon death, costs more for old out-of-shape smokers than for young trim non-smokers. Medical insurance, if there were such a thing, would do something similar.

Democratic government is inherently incapable of underwriting. That requires distinguishing between people, which is difficult for legislators who depend on them for votes. Legislating benefits for all is easier than apportioning responsibility or even acknowledging facts, such as our increasing lifespan as it applies to Social Security [30] benefits.

Group medical benefits provided by large employers are called insurance but are not a model for universal coverage by governments. While they do pay the costs of both routine and episodic care, participation is limited to a special group selected based on desirability for employment of at least one member of a family.[31] The cost is a part of the employee's compensation, which provides a regular source of funds. The cost may be controlled by having the medical service provided directly by a single enterprise, such as the Kaiser Foundation[32] Hospitals. And even these programs are coming under increasing pressure of rising costs.

Insurance clearly is not an appropriate model for publicly financing the full range of health care, but there may still be a role for market-based commercial insurance. For now though, let's examine a few specific problems with our current programs with an eye to making improvements that might help the market function better while preserving liberty.

Price Signals

Any free market depends on the signals provided by prices to inform both customers and providers of relative supply and demand. When these are not readily available the market is inefficient and prices are usually higher. For example, a Yale study[33] shows that in 2011 hospital prices for lower-limb MRIs were 12 times higher in the most expensive region of the United States (Bronx, New York) than in the cheapest region (Baltimore, Maryland) and could vary by up to a factor of 9 within the same city (e.g., Miami, Florida). Information like this is hard for individuals to obtain and is seldom even sought. Professional researchers have access,[34, 35] but consumers[36] are essentially unable to obtain this crucial information. Even a list of fixed cash prices at a local immediate care facility is daunting.[37] This is bad not only for the consumers, but it leaves many suppliers themselves in the dark about where they fit in the market.

Pharmaceutical Prices

Related to the service-price issue is that of well-hidden differentials in the price of pharmaceuticals. Import rules permit manufacturers to sell patent-protected drugs abroad at prices lower than they demand from domestic customers, and then prohibit re-importing these products, thus preserving monopoly pricing.

A possible remedy would be for the government to demand open pricing in return for patent protection. The customs wall that prohibits re-importing American made drugs should be a priority for repeal. There is no justification for government being complicit in monopoly pricing. Similar customers, in terms of quantity and other business factors, should be offered similar prices.

Liability

A perennial suggestion for reducing medical costs is to limit malpractice or tort liability. While the overall cost savings might not be large,[38] every bit helps. The same might be true for pharmaceuticals. Dozens of television commercials offer legal assistance in claiming damage from pills or devices. This cost is sure to be included in prices. Liability law should reflect the reality that new drugs and devices may cause harm undetected by even well-designed approval testing programs. So long as a manufacturer has honestly reported all test results, as well as those from continuous monitoring and responded appropriately, it should not be unduly liable for adverse results.

Medical Licensing

We must continue and expand the ongoing review and revision of medical licensing and practice requirements. Triage and routine care by physician's assistants or sub-professionals well trained in particular skills should allow fully qualified physicians to devote their justly highly compensated time to cases actually requiring their wide and deep knowledge and experience. For example, a local program[39] that sends paramedics without the ambulance to the homes of frequent 911 callers to assess and respond to their actual medical needs has cut emergency room visits in half.

Issues with the Affordable Care Act

As an exercise in seeing policy through the lens of liberty, let's consider a few issues that led to the current anger and anxiety over the Affordable Care Act and the possibility of its repeal. Enacted in 2010, it illustrates several ways not to try to solve the nation's health-care cost problem. Its structure is based on false principles and its enactment was based on deception.

Structural

The fundamental structural flaws in the ACA are that it forces people to pay for coverage they don't believe they need, and systematically shifts the cost between identifiable constituent groups. It is like forcing a person who doesn't own a car to pay for collision insurance or someone who lives remote from a source of rising water to buy flood insurance. An honest socialization scheme would raise funds through a general tax and cover everyone, but the ACA tries to obscure this principle by requiring everyone to buy a mislabeled "insurance" product. It forces people who take good care of themselves to pay for those who don't, raising the costs to the responsible citizens. Without going deeply into the details, here are examples of how and why it was based on simple economic or conceptual errors.

The ACA tries to cover hardship cases such as congenital conditions, addiction treatment, and the medically indigent by folding them into insurance required of everyone. This increases everyone's premiums, which forces more people to forgo insurance and so on in a death spiral.

Some legislators were persuaded to vote for it by requiring that adult children must be covered by their parents' policy up to the age of 26. The flaw here is that it continues and extends the underwriting error of adding an uncontrolled number of people to a "family" policy without increasing the premium. Each covered person obviously adds cost. If not, the benefit already would have been included. The cost to cover these twenty-somethings is shifted to couples with few or no children, and to those whose adult children support themselves. They are required to pay for a product for which they have no use or desire. Liberty loses. If an insurance company wants to do this for competitive reasons, fine. Just don't require it of everyone.

Another flaw is that the ACA was designed as a social benefit program rather than insurance. Maternity care might be a proper social objective but asking people unlikely to ever become pregnant to pay for it transforms insurance premiums into taxes without passing an honest tax increase. Similarly, people with little likelihood of becoming addicts are reluctant to pay for expensive drug treatment.

The term "pre-existing conditions" has been a hot-button issue in debating the ACA, with many meanings. Lumping them together into an ill-defined slogan was a recipe for conflict. No insurance company or public system should be expected to pay for a loss that has occurred or can reasonably be anticipated prior to entering into a contract. This is *adverse selection* or *gaming* the system. It describes potential clients who wait to obtain and pay for insurance until they either have had or expect soon to have a loss. You can't get fire insurance when you smell smoke, or flood insurance when the river is rising. Such fraudsters deserve no sympathy or subsidy. At the same time, people who have been responsible in caring for themselves yet contracted an expensive disease worry that circumstances might result in their losing an existing arrangement without the ability to gain coverage in another way.

The flaw is that legislators are neither able to determine the cost of adverse selection nor impose requirements on system gamers that would cover the true cost even if it could be known.

Enactment

Practically every rule of liberty and the Constitution was violated in enacting Obamacare. It takes property from some to give to others. Its passage was based on a combination of hubris, deception and willfully ignorant wishful thinking. It forces citizens to do things in which they do not believe. The ACA distorts language, and therefore thinking, when it labels what is basically a socialization program as insurance. Most important, there is no power enumerated in the Constitution to do anything like this in the first place.

Knowingly False Claims

The primary deception, violating the rule that I won't lie to or trick people, was a set of claims that promised lower costs and increased access to care. The true costs were obscured in a complex web of taxes, mandated purchases, and insurance policy provisions. Grand but knowingly false promises were made to garner political support.[40] For example, "The average family will save $2,500", and "If you like your doctor, you can keep him." The truth is that the typical family who already had insurance now pays more than before, not less.[41] Premiums for individual health care policies have doubled since 2013 according to an HHS report[42] released in May of 2017. While the amount is subject to many qualifications because of the interaction of innumerable parts, it is clearly large.[43]

Hidden Costs

Some people certainly gained increased access to medical care because of the passage of the ACA. They are visible, often vociferous, and now dependent on it, making the program almost impossible to eliminate. The ACA bureaucracy has probably counted every last one of them. No one, though, knows how many people have no job because a potential employer kept his headcount below 50, or whatever is the magic number to avoid the costs of Obamacare. We also don't know how many people have lost or could not obtain health insurance coverage, because that depends in a major way on definitions,[44] such as, is coverage lost when a policy is canceled but another more expensive one is offered?

Then, what else might have those who were taxed by stealth done with their money? This is an example of the different visibility between things done and not done,

Because the ACA relies on forced direct spending, its cost does not appear in the federal budget nor was it enacted as a tax. This is worse than taxation without representation. It is taxation without even identification.

Expiring Subsidies—Bait and Switch

Another consequence of the uncritical acceptance of the ACA is its impact on the Medicaid program for poor people, which is run by the states but subsidized by the federal government. Before passage of the ACA, the subsidy was in the form of partial matching funds, but the ACA provided 100% funding for a few years. The states opened their programs to all comers with this "free" money, but are now struggling as the subsidy is reduced, and fearful that it may fall even further.[45] Anyone looking closely knew that the full subsidy would not last forever, but the temptation was too great. Twice as many people enrolled as expected, and they now fear the loss of medical care. This was bait-and-switch on a massive scale.

Exceeding Congressional Capability

Congressional comity and effectiveness have suffered as well. Taking control of and managing one-fifth of the American economy is clearly an impossible task because of the vast amount of unknowable information affecting decisions every day by tens of millions of providers and consumers. The ACA attempted to codify this in some 2000 pages of legislation, including almost 3000 instances of "The Secretary shall determine." [46] The drafting was largely closed to most legislators and presented to them only a day before the vote. This led Republicans to chastise the Democrats for such duplicity, but when it became their turn to repeal it, they pursued the same tactic, proving the bipartisan nature of the dysfunction. One recent attempt[47] contains hundreds of sections. Another[48] is just as long, and its introduction seems just as opaque and full of improbable promises as the original passage. For example, a recent nominee for a cabinet position was heard to say something to the effect of "We want to provide the best possible care for everyone." This is impossible. Not everyone can have the best of anything. We can't all have a butler. Some arguments for repeal promise to eliminate the ACA taxes and mandates, and still provide everyone with "great" coverage at no cost. This also is patently impossible and reflects an unwillingness to honestly discuss the principles underlying the problem.

Had they read Hayek, they would have known better.

The purpose of government is to govern, not provide bread and circuses to the masses. However, the blame lies not with the politicians who propose unrealistic anti-liberty programs, but with the voters who fail to see the logical impossibility of their claims. The original proposal was wrong in principle.

A National Health Care Policy Consistent with Liberty

What would medical insurance respecting liberty look like? Here are some possibilities.

Underwriting

Insurance must be properly underwritten both to preserve its financial integrity and set premiums that appear fair and reasonable to policyholders. No one wants to buy insurance that covers losses they don't expect to incur or policyholders that practice risk management inferior to their own. People who eat healthily, exercise prudently and get plenty of sleep don't want to be in the same risk pool as overweight heavy-drinking smokers with high blood pressure.

As with underwriting risk, government is inherently almost incapable of imposing responsibility on voters. The best it has done is impose a small premium penalty on clients who wait too long to subscribe to the Medicare prescription drug program.[49] It cannot bring itself to tell an individual who smoked for years that this greatly increased his risk of lung cancer, or that the likelihood of developing diabetes is strongly linked to his high-fat diet, obesity and lack of exercise and therefore he must pay much more to insure against the risk of these diseases. A commercial insurance company should be able to do this, just as it rates other risks. The company, though, needs to know the risk factors of its clients and track these over time.

Life insurance companies require a physical exam prior to issuing a policy because they are loath to agree to pay a huge sum to the beneficiary of someone in bad shape after receiving only a few premium payments. A commercial medical insurance plan might require policyholders to obtain and pay for periodic physical exams and lab tests to determine factors known to affect future medical costs and base premium rates on the results. Government can assist by collecting massive amounts of data and providing it to insurance underwriters for developing commercial offerings. Any laws that restrict such underwriting would, of course, need to be repealed.

Beyond simply allowing insurance companies to accurately underwrite risks, the feedback to policyholders in the form of risk-based premiums should over time result in better health habits and lower overall health costs. If you know that your extra 50 pounds will cost you in premiums, you might do more walking and less eating.

One often hears the complaint that insurance companies care only about profit and don't care about people. Of course they care about profits, else they disappear. The same thing happens to one that treats policyholders noticeably worse than do its competitors. It's foolish to consider an insurance company as your friend or benefactor. It is a business with which you have a contractual agreement.

Policy Structure and Taxes

Just as insurance companies offer term and whole life policies, they should be able to offer short-term and lifetime medical policies based on their underwriting experience and financial ability. It's possible to envision a lifetime policy that incorporates requirements to maintain certain levels of personal condition in areas subject to self-control to retain a contractual level of premiums. The premiums could account for the general increase in medical use with age by either front loading or by planned contractual premium increases with time. It is dishonest to make insurance deny or cover up the facts of life.

There is no reason to buy insurance for routine expenses. It should cover only large, unpredictable events. Whether this is accomplished by high deductibles or a schedule of covered or excluded procedures should be left to insurers to offer and customers to choose.

A big step forward in normalizing the healthcare market would be for the government to equalize the tax treatment of health costs between buyers. At the very least, insurance purchased via an employer should be taxed the same as that purchased by an individual. There could even be favorable tax treatment for long-term saving for the predictable increase in medical costs with old age. That is, self-insurance by means of health savings accounts or something similar.

A modest improvement might be possible by facilitating the sale of medical insurance in a nationwide market. Is there really any justification for regulation of insurance by states? Could the federal government do a better job, at least for insurance sold in interstate commerce? Could it resist the temptation to dictate the contents of a medical insurance policy rather than just the safety and soundness of the issuing company? Government should still have a role in detecting and prosecuting fraud.

Pricing Transparency

Any government rules allowing or even requiring obscurity in prices should be repealed and replaced with firm requirements for open and clear pricing. Even now, a handful of medical providers are experimenting with published fixed prices.[50] Let us hope the trend continues.

The main difficulty with pricing medical services is there are so many and they are necessarily described in medical terminology, so means will have to be developed for, and patients must learn how to use, listings of standardized procedures. This might be a market opportunity for a smart-phone app that translates an individual's description of a medical problem into possible diagnoses, treatments, and costs. With reliable information about quality and prices, consumers should be able to do what they always do, that is, shop and compare, and providers will have useful information upon which to base plans for improvement.

Pre-Existing Conditions

People occasionally suffer a loss while adequately covered by insurance but then find they cannot renew their coverage or are charged high premiums after an illness, especially if some unrelated event, such as moving to another state, requires them to change insurers.

With automobile liability insurance, a string of accidents or an official determination of fault may indicate a true increase in risk warranting an increased premium or even cancellation of a policy. The rationale is that such experience is believed to be largely under the control of the individual. It may indicate careless driving habits.

Health insurance is different. First, as discussed above, health insurers should be allowed to rate client risk based on periodic physiological tests that measure general health and fitness. If a client with, for example, average health and fitness contracts a disease such as cancer, is treated appropriately, stabilizes suitably and continues to exhibit average fitness as appropriate to his condition, this should be considered normal experience and the risk of any potential future disease should have been incorporated in the original underwriting. The policy should neither be canceled nor premium increased because the risk of multiple occurrences should already be built in. If this is done right, even changing insurance companies should be possible with no significant increase in cost.

There will always be congenital pre-existing conditions outside anyone's control. People can be born with conditions that impose lifetime infirmity and cost. Some conditions may not even be detectable at birth, but the medical profession can recognize them when they manifest. These are candidates for socializing the cost through tax-based public premium support as needed. The cost would appear to be a tiny fraction of what is now spent. The understandable compassion for people suffering from such afflictions does not justify open-ended coverage of the entire population, or for health problems caused by lifestyle choices.

Chronic Conditions

A large part of the cost of publicly paid health care goes to supporting chronic conditions requiring intense expensive care. Kidney dialysis might be an example. If realistic underwriting based on suitable periodic exams detects precursors to such conditions* and motivates early lifestyle corrections through premiums reflecting the increased risk, responsible policyholders can be expected to make the personal changes leading not only to lower premiums but better health and less risk of developing these conditions in the first place. If they don't monitor and manage their own health, then continually increasing premiums should cover the costs. This is another way of saying that responsible people who care for their own good health and buy insurance early in their lives should benefit from that foresight.

The costs of chronic conditions that appear out of the blue with no warning from periodic tests or lifestyle assessment

---

* Rising hypertension might be an example.

215

would naturally be reflected in the overall experience of similarly situated policyholders and be built into premiums. Large random costs are exactly why we have insurance.

We could go deeper into the weeds of policy, underwriting, and personal responsibility, but the point is that most of the objective cost problems with pre-existing conditions can be resolved by permitting insurance companies to do real risk analysis and sell long-term policies based on that. The value of pursuing the subject as far as we have is that it illustrates the impossibility of crafting a uniform government plan to equitably cover all situations without crippling our republic's budget and doing violence to liberty.

Safety Net

Harkening back to our understanding that the American health care market is much too large and complex[51] ever to be satisfied by any central plan, including the reforms suggested here, we must face the certainty that some people will not have the medical care they desire. Some will be by choice or poor planning, but there may still be some who lack care for unforeseen reasons. As discussed earlier, this is not a legitimate federal responsibility, but states may decide to offer last-resort care in forms they deem suitable to their situations. High-risk pools might assist otherwise responsible people who have exhausted insurance coverage. It might make sense to establish bare-bones charity clinics to provide basic care directly to those who have foregone insurance or other forms of personal responsibility. Such a program should never be allowed to become the primary source of medical care for a large part of the population.

Health Care Summary

The fundamental flaw in any program to provide health care to the whole nation is that it is not governing, but personal life management. It's something that government cannot do well and which our government was never intended or designed to do. Providing an environment in which people can responsibly plan for and manage their own health will require that government mostly get out of the way but support a medical market with information and rules to keep it open and free. There could even be government support for very limited last-resort care. Here are some suggestions:

- Repeal all laws and regulations that restrict publication of prices for medical service or products.
- Repeal all laws and regulations that restrict or tax importation of American made pharmaceutical or medical products.
- Require by law that the prices for all transactions providing medical services or products be reported to the US Government for analysis and publication while protecting the privacy of individual patients.
- Direct the National Institutes of Health to develop, maintain and publish an up to date index of medical care services and procedures to facilitate dissemination of pricing data.
- Repeal all laws regulating the substantive content of medical insurance policies.
- Require by law all medical insurance policies to use coverage definitions standardized by a recognized industry group.
- Enact uniform regulations facilitating interstate commerce in medical insurance. Include standards and regulation of safety and soundness of insurance providers.
- Direct the National Institutes of Health to develop, maintain and publish standards of practice for testing new drugs and devices, and for collecting and publishing results. Amend tort laws to protect manufacturers who abide by these standards.
- Review and revise medical licensing and practice standards to facilitate paraprofessional patient care to the

greatest extent possible while maintaining reasonable quality.

- Repeal all laws and regulations entitling the general public to full medical care except for special circumstances such as epidemic control, disaster relief or as earned benefits of federal employment.

Unwinding government intrusion in a health care market serving the bulk of the public will not be easy but is necessary to preserve liberty. This does not deny the utility of states providing a small amount of basic last-resort medical care to a small fraction of the population through regular appropriations, not as individual entitlements. Reality and compassion demand we do something of this nature. Preservation of not just liberty but the soundness of our government requires that we proceed with prudence and awareness of government's limitations.

Epilogue

We've seen that liberty results from observing five simple rules for self-restraint. *I don't physically attack people except in self-defense. I don't take their stuff. I don't lie to or cheat them. I don't dump my garbage on their lawn.* And *I don't try to make them believe what I believe.* Most readers of this book probably follow these rules in their own lives whether they have thought much about them or not. Our message is that they are the best way for people to get along while living together in large groups, from neighborhoods to nations. They are also excellent criteria for judging government policy because a legitimate government has only powers delegated by the people, and the people can delegate only powers they possess. The rules of liberty specify which powers are excluded.

We have also seen that a strong government is needed to protect us from those who would violate liberty's rules. Such a government is necessarily sovereign over the entire State, so is in a good position to provide public goods that support civil society. Unfortunately, that power is a temptation to those who would use it for other agendas, such as equalizing the conditions of life or improving culture. Pursuing these agendas entails abandoning liberty. The result is a permanent tension between liberty and the force necessary to protect it. Reapplying the rules of liberty to government will reduce this tension and many of the ills afflicting our nation.

Liberty doesn't come with a guarantee. Constitutions and courts are important supports, but unless citizens hold clear principles, pay attention to government, and participate, liberty will be lost to apathy and the ambitions of its enemies. The author's hope for this book is that it helps us appreciate and defend the ideals essential to a free people.

Acknowledgments

The author lacks formal training in philosophy or political science but has benefited from contact with friends and colleagues who have exposed me to powerful concepts in both fields. My first real contact with governing was as a member, and sometime chairman, of the Planning Commission of the recently (1964) incorporated Town of Portola Valley in California while it was developing and applying land use rules. Our mentor was Town Attorney Jim Morton, who gave us seminars on the considerable powers of government, while drilling into us our obligation to respect constitutional rights as we exercised those powers. My longtime California friend and neighbor Marc Pasturel has patiently instructed me in modern progressivism with a Gallic flavor.

After retiring from my day job of applied engineering research and relocating to Southern Oregon, I joined a small group dedicated to discussing political philosophy. I want to thank current and recent members, Martin Seim, Bob Scheelen, Leon Guild, Jim Harleman, Dave Dotterrer, David Churchman, and Joe Charter for allowing me to see the world through the eyes of high school teachers, college professors, a state child-welfare manager, a US Marine colonel, and a judge. Their politics range from progressive liberal to mainline conservative. They and my daughter Alice Ames Jahn have all helped me refine my exposition of the principles and application of liberty. I am especially indebted to a former member, Dr. Gordon Dickerson, who introduced me to the principles of liberty, which I have augmented with my own perspectives.

This book would not have begun had not my wife, Janet Boggia, opened my eyes to the grand sweep of cosmological history. She is working to publish that story in three volumes.

She has generously and lovingly taken time from that massive project to point out the rough edges of excessive zeal in my manuscript.

A note to first-time authors: Sam (Samantha?) Wright, a "gig" editor at fiverr.com going by the nom-de-plume of samwrightwrites, improved on my sentence style. There is always something new to learn about that. Thank you.

I also owe a debt to Google, Wikipedia and hordes of generous people and institutions that have digitized sources and maintained web servers to make much of the background material cited here readily available to all.

Appendix A: Immigration Risks

Terrorism

To put the risk of terrorism in perspective, consider first some different causes of mortality, and the differences in how we react to them.

In 2010, 69,000 Americans died from diabetes,[1] in 2015 35,000 from automobile crashes.[2] In this same general period, annual deaths domestically from terrorist attacks, while subject to interpretation, were only in the tens[3,4] which would be a rounding error in the others. Does this mean we can neglect terrorism as a relatively insignificant problem? No. The difference is that we have personal control over the others, and their causes are impersonal. They do not result from the willful act of another. We all know that an unhealthy diet shortens our lives, yet the tradeoff is accepted if only unconsciously. We know that traveling is dangerous, but we do it because it brings a benefit.

Terrorism is a different threat from auto travel or diabetes. It is human evil. The terrorist singles out his victims and kills them on purpose. There is no rational adjustment we can make to our daily lives to reduce the threat, which is the whole point of terrorism. The only defense is to eliminate the source.

We go to great lengths to identify potential terrorists among those seeking asylum as refugees.[5] Whether the same measures are applied to other immigrant applicant classes is not clear. Some, like the San Bernardino murderers, slip through.[6] The measures we have rely heavily on data about known terrorist connections derived from home-country and intelligence sources. Our methods don't seem to give much weight to details of religious associations, which is what recently has been distinguishing most foreign-born terrorists.

Race and religion are sensitive topics. Moslems who regard Islam as a spiritual practice in the way religion is considered here should be as welcome as anybody. What we must reject are Sharia Supremacists[7] who believe in a totalitarian political ideology unalterably hostile to our principles. Does it make sense then to subject Moslems to greater scrutiny than Anglicans? Unfair, but yes. Can this be a perfect criterion for rejecting potential terrorists? No, but it may be the best we can do as part of a more comprehensive policy.

Pew polling shows just over half of Moslems living in the Middle East (It varies by country) categorically denounce such terrorist acts as suicide bombing.[8] The absolute percentages and distinctions between "often, sometimes, and rarely" are less important than the fact that the degree of acceptance is big enough to be measured. A different poll[9] by the Arab Center for Research and Policy Studies found that while only about ten percent of Arabs had at least a somewhat positive view of ISIS,[10] another thirteen percent had an only somewhat negative view. This 23%, even though a minority, is too large to ignore. This makes the majority of Middle Eastern Arabs passive uninvolved victims. While blameless themselves, they suffer from the natural need of countries such as the US to take strong measures to avoid admitting killers.

It's impossible to know the exact magnitude of this threat, but we can speculate well enough to develop policy. For example, we can hope that 95% of refugees in these broad categories are legitimate victims of events beyond their control and wish only to be left alone to live peaceful lives. Of the remaining 5% maybe most are nothing worse than common criminals. But some will be terrorists committed to killing as many Americans as possible. Maybe this is only 1% of the total. The problem is we can't identify this subset without a verifiable personal history from a friendly responsible government, the lack of which is exactly why most are refugees. Unsupported assertions to the contrary, this is simply impossible when we have large numbers of people facing a finite number of immigration agents.

Consider the task of assessing suitability for asylum, or "vetting" in the popular parlance, of 100,000 people about whom we can know little. Suppose we exert as much effort as we can. How many of my assumed 1% terrorists (1000 individuals) will be identified? Is it half, nine out of ten? Even the latter leaves a hundred possibly trained killers in our peaceful nation free to seek soft targets to commit mayhem.[11] Then there are the possibly four thousand common criminals. Maybe we'll identify half of these, maybe not. We don't know. They can do a lot of damage.[12] My assumed numbers are probably way off, either way. How confident can we be of this? Are there better-founded estimates? How do we know that? How much hurt could one terrorist with a stolen 20-ton truck inflict on a crowded mall in Des Moines or a small town Independence Day parade?

This has been a larger digression from the basic principles that should underlie our immigration policy than might seem warranted, but the problem of terrorism is real. Peaceful immigrants are to some extent victims along with our citizens who are killed or injured. Denying them entry does them an injustice, and we lose their energy, but that is unavoidable when we are unsure how to distinguish the good from the bad. Despite rationalizations by apologists for the terrorists, the threat demands government protection of our citizens. And we have only the tools we have, not what might be perfect.

Refugee Assimilation Hurdles

Crime and terrorist attacks kill specific people at specific times, but there may be a larger, longer-term cost to admitting large numbers of people from very different cultures who are attracted more to the immediate benefits of our safety and economy than to our culture. All refugees come from places with no experience of liberty as we in our founding ideals and better moments understand it here. They have no concept of a government created by free people which is itself governed by law that it cannot easily change, or of things we take for granted such as a secular state, freedom of speech, lack of widely accepted corruption, independence and civil rights for women, and peaceful transfer of power by honest elections. Even when not drawn to crime or terrorism, unassimilated refugees from incompatible cultures are prey to demagogues who emphasize their need to stick together and vote their identity. This may be why they appeal to collectivist and identity-group-oriented politicians. The refugee's natural need for social services reinforces their allegiance to such leaders.

There is no doubt that a few individuals integrated in small numbers into actively welcoming communities are able to learn, understand and appreciate American political and social culture. Expecting this to happen for large groups isolated by language, religion, and culture though is wishful thinking.[13] The adult refugees are mostly just thankful to be alive and able to live quietly. Their children, though, while American citizens if they were born here, are adrift in a strange land. They are isolated in language and religion ghettos, have not absorbed our culture, and theirs is diluted and distorted. They then fail to learn English and, more importantly, retain an outsider outlook which leaves them prey to radical separatist groups such as La Raza[14, 15] or even the Aztlan[16] movement. Terrorist and gang recruiters have a fertile field. Sometimes, their popular culture lionizes narco-terrorists.[17] We must be conscious of the European experience[18] and avoid it here.

Previous waves of refugees did not suffer such severe impediments to assimilation. The early Irish refugees from famine and oppression were at least Christian with a tradition of some degree of freedom. They spoke English. They wanted to become Americans despite discrimination. And they did. The Jewish refugees from Nazi genocide in the 1930s and 40s were in the main highly civilized well-educated Europeans with a well-developed sense of religious freedom. They either already spoke English or learned it quickly. Though often suffering cruel discrimination here, they quickly integrated to the extent possible. There were Armenian refugees from Turkish genocide. Many settled in southern California around Glendale,[19] quickly making a new life here and adopting our culture even to the extent of furnishing the state a governor. The Cubans who escaped the communist takeover of their country were Christians generally with professional and business backgrounds who while concentrating in Florida managed to fit right in as new Americans. My experience with them has been that they often understand and appreciate our liberty better than some native-born Americans.[20]

Asylum, while satisfying our urge to compassion, now has accrued significant potential costs partly because of the culture of some asylum seekers, as well as the sheer volume. We must dispassionately assess the costs vs. potential benefits to our civil society of admitting large numbers.

Weak Criteria

Family reunification[21] accounts for the largest category of legal immigration. It's based on the general principle of compassion but has become a loophole to bypass quotas based on the benefit to the United States. Costs similar to those evident in many of the recent asylum seekers are mounting. The policy should be reassessed to measure the actual benefits to the United States and appropriate changes enacted. Citizenship should be granted only to legal immigrants demonstrating full assimilation into our language and public culture. This won't be easy if many of our natural born citizens are unsure what that is.

Another potential criterion for developing or evaluating immigration policy is often expressed in terms of cultural relativism or multicultural equality. This is the idea that nothing is unique about our culture, so there is no reason to distinguish the United States from any other nation or people. It leads to the conclusion that national borders mean nothing,[22] so why enforce them. "It isn't fair that we live in a rich country while others are poor." The premise behind this line of reasoning is false because the principles on which the United States is organized are fundamentally different from and superior to those that control life in those parts of the world furnishing the most refugees and family reunification applicants. The contemporary corroding of our principles doesn't weaken this argument; it only shows the necessity for re-examining and reinforcing them.

Then there is the old chestnut of guilt for colonialism.[23] It's partly a belief that the West became rich by stealing resources from tropical peoples. Or, the West prevented colonized people from naturally developing vibrant economies and political cultures by conquering them and ruling from afar or by colluding with local tyrants to unfairly extract resources. In either case, the supposed remedy is reparations in the form of cash or citizenship. While there are bits of truth in these claims, they ignore the cultural and economic benefits available from association with western ideas of liberty, honest government, education, and technology. Some former colonies such as India have made better use of this than others. While there is a certain charm and integrity in a subsistence life, penicillin and clean water are probably better, and a government protecting liberty is better still.

There doesn't seem to be much reason to base our population, immigration, or citizenship policies on guilt. The best we can do for disadvantaged people around the world is provide a clear example of liberty, along with foreign student education and other exchanges that support its spread. The responsibility of our government is to our citizens, not to potential immigrants. We owe them nothing, no matter their individual merit. Residency and citizenship in America are privileges we may grant to foreigners, not a right.

Improving the quality of life in the United States is obviously in our national interest. Technology in a free market economy has produced enough food and shelter for our population as it has expanded from a colonial agricultural and Native American hunter-gatherer beginning to some 300 million mostly well-fed and comfortable urban people, so we need not fear a Malthusian[24] limit to our population. We send a few more tens of billions of dollars' worth of agricultural products abroad than we import, in a total trade of over 100 billion dollars a year,[25] though recently our agricultural surplus has diminished.

Population Pressure

There are, though, serious indicators of overpopulation, and thus a decrease in quality of life. The first, more objective, indicator is the difficulty of providing sufficient pure water for direct use by people and by the economy on which our good life depends. In one study, 40 of 50 state water managers expected shortages in some portion of their state under average conditions in the next 10 years.[26] While there are technical means for purifying sea water, they use massive amounts of energy, which is not only costly but has its own impact on quality of life, including consuming lots of water.[27] Keeping the air clean is also becoming more expensive, as we learn from the costs of producing so-called clean coal.[28]

Then there is the subjective matter of simple crowding. It manifests directly as road congestion, the anonymity of living in high-rise apartments, and the difficulty of finding space in cities to experience solitude in nature. It requires special effort, which many urban dwellers don't make, to give children the experience of nature except in manicured parks and similar places. As more people live closer together, more rules and restrictions are necessary to maintain some semblance of peace and even clean air. Population density in many areas means giving up wood stoves as an economical, independent, and cheerful way to heat a house.[29] None of this contributes to fostering the kind of independent citizen who values liberty.

Indirect effects of an increasing global population appear in many ways. For example, we are hearing that the earth can't support enough pasture land to provide steak or even fresh vegetables for everyone, and we will all eventually be eating processed algae and insects. I, for one, don't feel that's a good trade for any benefits of a larger population. Why not live in a world that is comfortable and gracious for a few billion people rather than a constricted one for ten times that many?

End Notes

These notes contain numerous internet Universal Resource Locators (URLs). They were all functional when collected, but some may become inactive or possibly garbled in the transition to print. Googling key words from the URL or the main text should reach equally informative material.

Chapter 1 What is Liberty?

[1] I first saw this expression of liberty in an informal piece by David Boaz of the Cato Institute. Mine is expanded a bit. Boaz also offers a comprehensive history and exposition of liberty in *The Libertarian Mind*, Simon and Schuster, New York 2015.

[2] https://islamqa.info/en/20327

[3] http://www.dailymail.co.uk/news/article-3583507

Chapter 2 What Liberty is Not

[1] https://www.ftc.gov/tips-advice/competition-guidance/guide-antitrust-laws

[2] https://www.cato.org/policy-report/mayjune-2018/big-techs-big-time-big-scale-problem

[3] http://www.nationalreview.com/article/434549/left-western-civilization-case-hatred

Chapter 3 The Value of Liberty

[1] The ancient Greeks developed ideas of how to rule justly. The assumption, though, was that there had to be a ruler. They invented democracy to solve the problem of who should select the ruler, and how. This was far from liberty as we understand it. In a seemingly endless series of wars among themselves and their neighbors, they for a time held territory as far away as India. Unfortunately, they lost both their conquests and democracy for many centuries.

[2] *Self-Reliance and Other Essays*, 1993, Dover Publications

[3] Palmer, Tom G., *Self-Control or State Control – You Decide*, Jameson Books, Inc, Ottawa, Illinois, 2016

[4] Palmer, Ton G, *Why Liberty – Your Life, Your Choices, Your Future*, Jameson Books Inc, Ottawa, Illinois, 2013
[5] Stephen E. Lucas, "Justifying America: The Declaration of Independence as a Rhetorical Document", in Thomas W. Benson, ed., *American Rhetoric: Context and Criticism*, Southern Illinois University Press, Carbondale, Illinois,1989, p. 85
[6] Joseph J. Ellis, *American Creation: Triumphs and Tragedies in the Founding of the Republic*, Alfred A. Knopf/Random House (NY/Toronto), 2007
[7]https://en.wikipedia.org/wiki/United_States_Declaration_of_Independence
[8] https://theconversation.com/emergence-the-remarkable-simplicity-of-complexity-30973
[9] https://en.wikipedia.org/wiki/Chronology_of_the_universe is a compact time history of the physical processes mentioned here.
[10] See https://www.cfa.harvard.edu/~ejchaisson/cosmic_evolution/docs/splash.html for a web-based summary from Harvard. Note that some of the videos have no sound.
[11] https://en.wikipedia.org/wiki/Abiogenesis
[12] https://en.wikipedia.org/wiki/Snail_darter_controversy

Chapter 4 Governing for Liberty

[1] Francis Fukuyama, *The Origins of Political Order*, Farrar, Straus and Giroux, 2011
[2] https://en.wikipedia.org/wiki/German_town_law
[3] https://en.wikipedia.org/wiki/Magna_Carta
[4] https://en.wikiquote.org/wiki/Henry_Kissinger
[5] https://www.nytimes.com/2014/06/27/nyregion/city-loses-final-appeal-on-limiting-sales-of-large-sodas.html
[6] https://en.wikipedia.org/wiki/Inauguration_of_John_F._Kennedy
[7] http://www.people-press.org/2017/05/03/public-trust-in-government-remains-near-historic-lows-as-partisan-attitudes-shift/
[8] https://ij.org/ll/june-2018-volume-27-issue-3/
[9] The quote is buried in a long essay at http://www.nationalreview.com/g-file/456286/ideology-trump-white-house-rob-porter-wife-abuse

Chapter 5 The Constitution

[1] https://www.constitutionfacts.com/us-articles-of-confederation/the-great-debate/
[2] *The American Heritage Illustrated Encyclopedic Dictionary*, Houghton Mifflin Company, Boston 1987
[3] https://en.wikipedia.org/wiki/Timeline_of_drafting_and_ratification_of_the_United_States_Constitution

[4] https://www.archives.gov/founding-docs/bill-of-rights-transcript

[5] http://www.heritage.org/constitution/#!/articles/6/essays/133/supremacy-clause

[6] http://constitutionus.com/

[7] http://www.stateoftheunionhistory.com/2017/12/1824-james-monroe-federal-funding-of.html

[8] http://www.nationalreview.com/article/444759/ninth-amendment-rights-protection

[9] http://www.nationalreview.com/article/444798/ninth-circuit-travel-ban-decision-united-states-constitution-unalienable-rights-privileges-alexander-hamilton

[10] http://rationalwiki.org/wiki/Roe_v._Wade

[11] https://www.supremecourt.gov/opinions/07pdf/07-290.pdf

[12] http://www.nationalreview.com/article/456282/border-patrol-warrantless-searches-often-unconstitutional

[13] http://www.law.uchicago.edu/alumni/magazine/fall10/strauss

[14] http://www.taxhistory.org/thp/readings.nsf/ArtWeb/736DB4705B4EE21D85256F2B00548FA3?OpenDocument

[15] https://en.wikipedia.org/wiki/Eighteenth_Amendment_to_the_United_States_Constitution

[16] https://www.forbes.com/sites/kellyphillipserb/2012/06/28/when-is-a-penalty-a-tax-sorting-through-the-scotus-health-care-decision/#3a92f83d5bf3

[17] https://www.theatlantic.com/business/archive/2012/06/the-tiny-distinction-that-saved-obamacare-why-the-penalty-is-a-tax/259140/

[18] https://en.wikipedia.org/wiki/Wickard_v._Filburn

[19] http://tenthamendmentcenter.com/2010/08/13/is-social-security-constitutional/

[20] https://scholarship.law.duke.edu/cgi/viewcontent.cgi?article=1197&context=djglp

Chapter 6 Full-Service Government with Liberty

[1] https://en.wikipedia.org/wiki/Rod_Blagojevich_corruption_charges#Sentence

[2] https://www.archives.gov/founding-docs/constitution-transcript#toc-section-2--2

[3] https://en.wikipedia.org/wiki/Right_to_keep_and_bear_arms_in_the_United_States

[4] https://www.archives.gov/founding-docs/constitution-transcript Article I, Section 8.

[5] https://www.nationalreview.com/2004/07/core-gap-map-mackubin-thomas-owens/

6 https://www.amazon.com/Why-We-Fight-Management-Conflict/dp/0761861378/ref=sr_1_6
7 https://fas.org/sgp/crs/secrecy/RS20748.pdf
8 http://thefederalistpapers.org/us/what-the-founders-said-about-moralitys-role-in-maintaining-republican-government
9 http://www.nationalreview.com/article/449018/california-where-separatism-finds-home
10
https://www.heritage.org/constitution/#!/articles/4/essays/126/property-clause
11 https://elr.info/sites/default/files/articles/20.10003.htm
12 Ayn Rand, *Atlas Shrugged*, New York: Random House, 1957, and New York, Signet, 1959 p. 964, or p. 136 of Leonard Peikoff, *Objectivism: The Philosophy of Ayn Rand*, Penguin/Meridian, 1991.
13 https://www.washingtonpost.com/news/capital-weather-gang/wp/2016/06/09/congress-is-considering-privatizing-key-roles-of-the-weather-service-thats-a-mistake
14 http://www.redding.com/story/news/2017/05/23/farmer-faces-2-8-million-fine-plowing-field/336407001/
15 https://en.wikipedia.org/wiki/Paris_Agreement
16 Adapted from The Lives of the Constitution, by Joseph Tartakovsky, Encounter Press, 2018, reviewed by Jay Cost, National Review, April 30, 2018
17 https://www.uscis.gov/history-and-genealogy/our-history/agency-history/early-american-immigration-policies
18 *"Give me your tired, your poor,*
Your huddled masses yearning to breathe free,
The wretched refuse of your teeming shore.
Send these, the homeless, tempest-tost to me,
I lift my lamp beside the golden door!"
The closing lines of the plaque on the Statue of Liberty, by Emma Lazarus, November 2, 1883
https://www.nps.gov/stli/learn/historyculture/colossus.htm
19 http://news.nationalgeographic.com/news/2013/06/130630-immigration-reform-world-refugees-asylum-canada-japan-australia-sweden-denmark-united-kingdom-undocumented-immigrants/
20 https://en.wikipedia.org/wiki/Immigration_by_country
21 http://newobserveronline.com/saudi-arabias-racial-immigration-laws/
22 https://www.mercatus.org/publication/how-many-workers-support-one-social-security-retiree
23 http://www.hcd.ca.gov/housing-policy-development/housing-resource-center/plan/he/heoverview.pdf

[24] Daniel Hannan, *Inventing Freedom – How the English-Speaking Peoples Made the Modern World*, Harper Collins, 2013

[25] https://en.wikipedia.org/wiki/American_Immigration_Lawyers_Association

[26] https://en.wikipedia.org/wiki/Immigration_to_the_United_States

[27] http://cis.org/sites/cis.org/files/camarota-illegal-pop-growth_1.pdf

[28] http://www.oregonlive.com/politics/index.ssf/2015/11/oregon_driver_cards_immigrants.html

[29] https://openborders.info/human-smuggling-fees/

[30] https://www.uscis.gov/tools/glossary/permanent-resident-alien

[31] http://www.americanbar.org/publications/gp_solo/2011/april_may/immigration_law_aprimer.html

[32] https://www.americanimmigrationcouncil.org/research/guide-children-arriving-border-laws-policies-and-responses

[33] http://cis.org/Welcoming-Unaccompanied-Alien-Children-to-the-United-States

[34] http://www.nytimes.com/2012/12/01/us/dream-act-gives-young-immigrants-a-political-voice.html

[35] http://www.oregonlive.com/pacific-northwest-news/index.ssf/2016/11/ashland_police_department_on_f.html

[36] https://en.wikipedia.org/wiki/Sanctuary_city

[37] https://en.wikipedia.org/wiki/Alien_(law)

[38] https://travel.state.gov/content/travel/en/legal-considerations/us-citizenship-laws-policies/citizenship-child-born-abroad.html So what was all the fuss about Barack Obama? His mother was a US Citizen, so it doesn't matter where he was born.

[39] https://en.wikipedia.org/wiki/Birthright_citizenship_in_the_United_States

[40] http://cis.org/birthright-citizenship

[41] https://www.uscis.gov/sites/default/files/USCIS/Office%20of%20Citizenship/Citizenship%20Resource%20Center%20Site/Publications/100q.pdf

[42] http://www.latimes.com/opinion/op-ed/la-oe-hanson-borders-20160731-snap-story.html

[43] https://www.youtube.com/watch?v=wSA5CK_ipnE

[44] http://www.nationalreview.com/article/454591/child-poverty-rates-america-why-we-cannot-lower-them

[45] This research shows the remarkable increase in democracy over the past half century.
http://www.hh.se/images/18.341e6abb148eccb76f5369b/1412840411980/MaxRange+Poster.png

---

[46] https://www.nytimes.com/2017/06/28/opinion/canada-immigration-policy-trump.html?emc=edit_th_20170628&nl=todaysheadlines&nlid=20976618
[47] https://en.wikipedia.org/wiki/Boston_Marathon_bombing
[48] https://en.wikipedia.org/wiki/Bracero_program
[49] http://www.oregonloggers.org/Forest_facts_HarvestData.aspx
[50] https://transition.fcc.gov/Reports/1934new.pdf
[51] https://en.wikipedia.org/wiki/Spectrum_auction
[52]
https://en.wikipedia.org/wiki/Occupation_of_the_Malheur_National_Wildlife_Refuge
[53] http://la.lawsoup.org/legal-guides/laws-by-topic/sidewalks-public-spaces/
[54] https://en.wikipedia.org/wiki/Aggressive_panhandling
[55] These charts presented in a Congressional hearing are all you want to know about entitlement spending. https://judiciary.house.gov/wp-content/uploads/2016/06/Eberstadt-PPT-07062016.pdf
[56] http://www.law.harvard.edu/faculty/hjackson/auth_appro_15.pdf See especially page 22.
[57] Figure 16 in Nicholas Eberstadt, *A Nation of Takers – America's Entitlement Epidemic*, Templeton Press 2012
[58] https://www.forbes.com/sites/merrillmatthews/2014/07/02/weve-crossed-the-tipping-point-most-americans-now-receive-government-benefits/#621877ef3e6c
[59] https://www.washingtonpost.com/news/wonk/wp/2012/09/18/who-receives-benefits-from-the-federal-government-in-six-charts
[60] https://www.thoughtco.com/us-farm-subsidies-3325162
[61] http://www.redstate.com/patterico/2017/01/20/noooooooooooooooo-distraught-protester-screams-trump-inaugurated-video/
[62] There is a story, often told, that upon exiting the Constitutional Convention Benjamin Franklin was approached by a group of citizens asking what sort of government the delegates had created. His answer was: "A republic, if you can keep it."
 See http://constitutioncenter.org/learn/educational-resources/historical-documents/perspectives-on-the-constitution-a-republic-if-you-can-keep-it for an informative discussion.
[63] Go ahead, look it up.Here https://www.constituteproject.org/constitution/United_States_of_America_1992 is a convenient copy of the US Constitution. The powers granted to Congress are in Article 1, Section 8. You will find nothing granting Congress the power to tax some people for the personal benefit of others. And don't look to the old canard of the Constitution being out of date. Such a power would be general enough to have been included in the wording in 1887.

236

64 https://en.wikipedia.org/wiki/Hull_House

65 https://fee.org/articles/friendly-societies-voluntary-social-security-and-more/

66 Florence Leona Christie photographed by Dorothea Lange at a pea-picker's camp in California
http://mashable.com/2016/06/12/migrant-mother/#EqUXixv3ZkqW
http://www.eyewitnesstohistory.com/migrantmother.htm

67 http://www.heritage.org/research/reports/2014/09/the-war-on-poverty-after-50-years

68 A compact critique of the welfare state can be found in Tom G. Palmer (editor) *After the Welfare State*, Students for Liberty & Atlas Network/Jameson Books, Ottawa, Illinois, 2012

69 Charles Murray, *Coming Apart – The State of White America, 1960-2010* , Penguin Random House 2013

70 Myron Magnet, *The Dream and the Nightmare*, William Morrow & Co 1993

71
https://www.washingtonpost.com/news/parenting/wp/2015/09/01/everyones-a-winner-and-other-lies

72 http://www.nationalreview.com/article/440758/nicholas-eberstadts-men-without-work-american-males-who-choose-not-work

73 Nicholas Eberstadt, *Men Without Work*, Templeton Press 2016.
https://www.templetonpress.org/book/men-without-work

74 Table 4 in https://www.bls.gov/opub/mlr/2002/05/art2full.pdf

75 Withdrawal from work is analyzed in detail in Nicholas Eberstadt, *A Nation of Takers – America's Entitlement Epidemic*, Templeton Press, 2012

76 https://www.commentarymagazine.com/articles/our-miserable-21st-century/

77https://en.wikipedia.org/wiki/Personal_Responsibility_and_Work_Opportunity_Act

78 http://apps.npr.org/unfit-for-work/

79 This idea has been floated by Charles Murray, but so far only in the form of an essay in the Wall Street Journal, which is not accessible except by subscription. The best summary I could find is at
http://johnhcochrane.blogspot.com/2016/06/universal-basic-income.html .

80 https://www.nytimes.com/2018/04/24/business/finland-universal-basic-income.html

81 http://www.orencass.com/sites/default/files/160627-The%20End%20of%20Work%20(NR).pdf

82 Averaged over a full life, each year of work needs to create enough wealth to support one person that year plus one additional year, a 2–to–1 ratio. This big–picture view applies to everyone whether wage earner or homemaker, though the forms of productive work and saving may differ. From an overall

economic perspective, it doesn't matter if the 2–to–1 ratio is achieved by personal savings and child rearing or by inter–generational transfers.

[83] http://dailysignal.com/2017/02/15/4-broken-obamacare-promises-that-town-hall-protesters-should-remember/

[84] http://www.nytimes.com/2015/11/03/health/death-rates-rising-for-middle-aged-white-americans-study-finds.html?_r=0

[85] https://object.cato.org/sites/cato.org/files/pubs/pdf/ssp4.pdf

[86] Jeremy J. Siegel, *Stocks for the Long Run, Fifth Edition*, McGraw Hill, New York 2014 has been called "One of the ten best investment books of all time" by the Washington Post.

[87] https://www.tiaa.org/public/index.html

[88] http://www.reuters.com/article/us-usa-economy-jobs-idUSKCN11D1UX

[89] https://en.wikipedia.org/wiki/Cabrini%E2%80%93Green_Homes

[90] http://www.stvincentdepaulmedford.info/

[91] https://en.wikipedia.org/wiki/Homeboy_Industries

[92] http://www.latimes.com/opinion/op-ed/la-oe-boyle-kinship-20171128-story.html

[93] https://rwdcw.wordpress.com/

[94] https://mlf.org/community-first/ , and http://mailtribune.com/opinion/guest-opinions/a-bustling-oasis-serves-the-homeless-in-texas

[95] http://apps.npr.org/unfit-for-work/

[96] https://livingopps.org/about/

[97] http://www.thirdway.org/memo/where-are-the-job-offers

[98] http://onesourcerelocation.com/reluctance-to-relocate-top-reasons-why-employees-want-to-stay-where-they-are/

[99] Medford (Oregon) Mail Tribune, June 11,2017 "OnTrack Loses … Grant", http://www.mailtribune.com/news/20170611/ontrack-loses-control-of-19-million-state-grant

[100] https://www.ffiec.gov/cra/ , https://www.federalreserve.gov/communitydev/cra_about.htm,

[101] http://www.businessinsider.com/the-cra-debate-a-users-guide-2009-6

[102] https://en.wikipedia.org/wiki/Oil_depletion_allowance

[103] https://en.wikipedia.org/wiki/Carried_interest

[104] https://en.wikipedia.org/wiki/Patient_Protection_and_Affordable_Care_Act

[105] http://www.nationalreview.com/article/420144/kelo-eminent-domain-richard-epstein

[106] https://en.wikipedia.org/wiki/Wickard_v._Filburn

[107] http://www.hoover.org/research/feds-depression-and-birth-new-deal

[108] https://en.wikipedia.org/wiki/Humphrey%E2%80%93Hawkins_Full_Employment_Act

[109] https://www.federalreserve.gov/faqs/economy_14400.htm
[110] http://theeconomiccollapseblog.com/archives/11-reasons-why-the-federal-reserve-should-be-abolished
[111] http://www.marketwatch.com/story/what-would-happen-if-we-shut-down-the-federal-reserve-2016-05-24
[112] https://www.mobilepaymentstoday.com/articles/mobile-payments-help-swedens-move-to-a-cashless-society/
[113] http://wadhwa.com/2017/01/23/u-s-can-learn-indias-move-toward-cashless-society/
[114]

https://en.wikipedia.org/wiki/List_of_Nobel_Memorial_Prize_laureates_in_Economics
[115] This delusion is explored in detail by a man who was there in a responsible position. John A. Allison, *The Financial Crisis and the Free Market Cure – How Destructive Banking Reform Is Killing the Economy*, McGraw Hill, 2013
[116] See http://www.nationalreview.com/article/441691/conservatism-cronyism-policy-solutions-right for a more complete discussion of cronyism.
[117] https://en.wikipedia.org/wiki/Economy_of_the_Soviet_Union
[118] F.A. Hayek, *The Road to Serfdom – Text and Documents, The Definitive Edition*, edited by Bruce Caldwell, The University of Chicago Press, 2007.
[119] https://en.wikipedia.org/wiki/Lobbying_in_the_United_States
[120] https://www.swp-berlin.org/fileadmin/contents/products/comments/2017C05_nll.pdf
[121] https://en.wikipedia.org/wiki/Magna_Carta
[122] https://www.opendemocracy.net/od-russia/vladimir-gelman/russia%e2%80%99s-crony-capitalism-swing-of-pendulum
[123] https://www.amazon.com/Chinas-Entrepreneurial-Studies-Contemporary-China/dp/0199246904/ref=sr_1_1?s=books&ie=UTF8&qid=1480887111&sr=1-1&keywords=china+entrepreneurial+army
[124] https://www.revealnews.org/article/in-the-rural-west-residents-choose-low-taxes-over-law-enforcement/
[125] http://www.huffingtonpost.com/2012/06/28/supreme-court-health-care-decision_n_1585131.html
[126]

https://en.wikipedia.org/wiki/National_Federation_of_Independent_Business_v._Sebelius
[127] https://www.oyez.org/cases/2011/11-393
[128] https://www.brainyquote.com/quotes/quotes/r/russellbl101810.html
[129]

https://en.wikipedia.org/wiki/From_each_according_to_his_ability,_to_each_according_to_his_needs

130 http://www.politicalaffairs.net/you-might-be-a-marxist-if-you-believe-in-from-each-according-to-their-abilities-to-each-according-to-their-needs/
131 https://en.wikipedia.org/wiki/No_taxation_without_representation
132 https://en.wikipedia.org/wiki/Excise_tax_in_the_United_States
133 https://en.wikipedia.org/wiki/Taxation_history_of_the_United_States
134 http://www.washingtonexaminer.com/look-at-how-many-pages-are-in-the-federal-tax-code/article/2563032
135 https://www.federalreserve.gov/faqs/money_12848.htm
136 https://www.goodreads.com/author/quotes/198468.Margaret_Thatcher
137 https://www.nationalreview.com/2018/10/national-debt-solutions-will-be-painful/
138 https://www.nationalreview.com/2018/06/online-sales-tax-supreme-court-ruling-make-congress-act
139 http://knowledgecenter.csg.org/kc/system/files/Table_3.26.pdf
140
https://en.wikipedia.org/wiki/Emergency_Medical_Treatment_and_Active_Labor_Act
141 http://www.hhnmag.com/articles/5010-the-law-that-changed-everything-and-it-isn-t-the-one-you-think
142 https://www.hrsa.gov/gethealthcare/affordable/hillburton/
143 https://www.theatlantic.com/business/archive/2016/10/court-rules-consumer-financial-protection-bureaus-structure-is-unconstitutional/503660/

Chapter 7 Politics of Liberty

1 http://www.un.org/en/universal-declaration-human-rights/
2 Rand, Ayn, *Atlas Shrugged*, Random House, New York,1957 (Signet 1959)
3
http://xroads.virginia.edu/~ma98/pollklas/thesis/documents/federalistX.html
4 https://www.**cato**.org/
5 Tom G. Palmer, *Realizing Freedom – Libertarian Theory, History, and Practice*, CATO Institute, 2009 is an excellent exhaustive summary and exposition of libertarianism.
6 http://www.nationalreview.com/article/451267/leftism-liberalism-have-almost-nothing-common

Chapter 8 Contrary Principles

1 https://www.newclairvaux.org/who-we-are
2 https://en.wikipedia.org/wiki/Kibbutz
3 (Speech before the Chamber of Deputies, May 26, 1927, Discorsi del 1927, Milano, Alpes, 1928, p. 157)
http://www.worldfuturefund.org/wffmaster/Reading/Germany/mussolini.htm in footnote 8.

[4] http://www.history.com/topics/labor
[5] Edward J. Bacciocco, *The New Left in America – Reform to Revolution 1956-1970*, Hoover Institution Press, Stanford University, Stanford, California 1974
[6] http://www.heritage.org/political-process/report/woodrow-wilson-godfather-liberalism
[7] http://www.nytimes.com/2010/01/15/opinion/15brooks.html
[8]
https://en.wikipedia.org/wiki/From_each_according_to_his_ability,_to_each_according_to_his_needs
[9] https://en.wikipedia.org/wiki/New_Soviet_man
[10] https://en.wikipedia.org/wiki/Master_race
[11] http://www.sfgate.com/opinion/article/Eugenics-and-the-Nazis-the-California-2549771.php
[12] https://history.hanover.edu/courses/excerpts/111stalin.html
[13] http://news.stanford.edu/2010/09/23/naimark-stalin-genocide-092310/
[14] https://en.wikipedia.org/wiki/Reeducation_camp
[15] http://www.chicagotribune.com/news/opinion/commentary/ct-obamacare-saved-my-life-perspec-0113-20170111-story.html
[16] http://www.americanscientist.org/issues/feature/1999/2/early-canid-domestication-the-farm-fox-experiment/1
[17] https://en.wikipedia.org/wiki/Neoteny_in_humans
[18] https://en.wikipedia.org/wiki/Eloi
[19] http://www.moneycrashers.com/fair-tax-act-explained-pros-cons/
[20] http://www.fairimpartialpolicing.com/
[21]
https://portal.hud.gov/hudportal/HUD?src=/program_offices/fair_housing_equal_opp/FHLaws/yourrights
[22] http://fairelectionsnetwork.com/about/
[23] http://www.ferris.edu/jimcrow/what.htm
[24] http://www.washington.edu/news/2011/10/07/babies-show-sense-of-fairness-altruism-as-early-as-15-months/
[25] http://oliveremberton.com/2014/the-problem-isnt-that-life-is-unfair-its-your-broken-idea-of-fairness/
[26] http://www.heritage.org/research/reports/2014/08/john-rawls-theorist-of-modern-liberalism
[27] http://tinybuddha.com/blog/life-isnt-always-fair-5-steps-to-accept-tough-situations/
[28] http://www.forbes.com/sites/mikemyatt/2011/12/12/life-isnt-fair-deal-with-it/#242a50995d8d
[29] https://www.nytimes.com/2016/12/17/opinion/sunday/one-way-not-to-be-like-trump.html?_r=1
[30] https://en.wikipedia.org/wiki/Populism

31 http://dailysignal.com/2017/02/27/how-woodrow-wilson-planted-the-seeds-of-the-administrative-state/
32 http://scholarship.law.duke.edu/cgi/viewcontent.cgi?article=3075&context=dlj
33 https://lawblog.justia.com/2012/05/21/chevron-deference-your-guide-to-understanding-two-of-todays-scotus-decisions/
34 http://www.nationalreview.com/article/444477/donald-trump-supreme-court-nominee-neil-gorsuch-protects-constitutional-liberties
35 https://en.wikipedia.org/wiki/Confucianism#Women_in_Confucian_thought
36 https://www.bostonglobe.com/news/politics/2014/12/09/mit-professor-jonathan-gruber-apologizes-congress-for-remarks-about-stupidity-american-voter/AlrfLb2yWKWNTL9OvSaPFJ/story.html
37 https://www.regence.com/web/regence_individual/non-discrimination
Scroll down to see the list. Imagine what this costs to accommodate, and how isolated the clients must feel.
38 http://www.nationalreview.com/article/442792/ethnic-identity-politics-obama-administration-give-it-one-last-shot
39 http://www.ushistory.org/us/45d.asp
40 https://charlesohalloranboyd.wordpress.com/2013/10/05/woodrow-wilson-and-the-19th-amendment/
41 https://en.wikipedia.org/wiki/International_Civil_Aviation_Organization
42 https://en.wikipedia.org/wiki/Multiculturalism

Chapter 9 Religion

1 http://www.goodreads.com/quotes/699548-don-t-do-unto-others-what-you-don-t-want-others-to
2 http://www.jewishvirtuallibrary.org/jsource/Quote/hillel.html
3 http://www.thegoldenrule.net/quotes.htm
4 Alec Ryrie, *Protestants: The Faith That Made the Modern World*, Viking 2017, https://books.google.com/books/about/Protestants.html?id=VwzsDAAAQBAJ

Chapter 10 Liberty and Tough Issues

1 https://en.wikipedia.org/wiki/Rosa_Parks
2 https://en.wikipedia.org/wiki/Civil_Rights_Act_of_1964
3 https://en.wikipedia.org/wiki/Voting_Rights_Act_of_1965
4 https://www.archives.gov/education/lessons/woman-suffrage
5 http://usacac.army.mil/CAC2/MilitaryReview/Archives/English/MilitaryReview_20150430_art010.pdf

6 http://www.denverpost.com/2015/08/13/court-lakewood-baker-who-refused-gay-wedding-cake-cant-cite-beliefs/
7 http://www.simonandschuster.com/books/It-Takes-a-Village/Hillary-Rodham-Clinton/9781416540649
8 https://pencanada.ca/blog/free-expression-matters-hate-speech-in-canada-bill-59/
9 https://www.nationalreview.com/2018/04/canada-laws-crack-down-on-hate-speech
10 http://reason.com/blog/2015/01/02/katie-hopkins-illegal-tweeting
11 https://en.wikipedia.org/wiki/Censorship_in_the_United_Kingdom
12 http://www.newsweek.com/2016/06/03/college-campus-free-speech-thought-police-463536.html
13 https://www.nationalreview.com/2018/03/a-new-campus-survey-reveals-just-how-students-are-unlearning-liberty/
14 https://www.nytimes.com/2017/09/13/opinion/berkeley-dean-erwin-chemerinsky.html
15 https://www.theatlantic.com/politics/archive/2016/03/the-glaring-evidence-that-free-speech-is-threatened-on-campus/471825/
16 A 2018 report on US universities. https://www.thefire.org/spotlight-on-speech-codes-2018/
17 https://www.washingtonpost.com/outlook/students-think-they-can-suppress-speech-because-colleges-treat-them-like-customers/
18 http://www.nationalreview.com/article/451473/free-speech-princeton-constitution-day-lecture
19 https://stanfordreview.org/antifa-thugs-find-a-champion-and-leader-in-stanford-professor-3/
20 https://www.professorwatchlist.org/
21 https://en.wikipedia.org/wiki/Paris_Agreement
22 http://www.washingtontimes.com/news/2016/jun/2/calif-bill-prosecutes-climate-change-skeptics/
23 http://www.nationalreview.com/article/447196/march-science-touts-public-policy-choices-outside-scope-science
24 http://www.nationalreview.com/article/444480/neil-gorsuch-united-states-supreme-court-second-amendment-police-seizure-gun
25 https://www.cms.gov/research-statistics-data-and-systems/statistics-trends-and-reports/nationalhealthexpenddata/nationalhealthaccountshistorical.html
26 https://www.hhs.gov/sites/default/files/ppacacon.pdf
27 http://hcao.org/our-mission/
28 http://healthblog.ncpa.org/why-cant-the-market-for-medical-care-work-like-cosmetic-surgery/#sthash.NOqL00mU.dpbs
29 http://www.medicaltourismassociation.com/en/medical-tourism-faq-s.html

---

30
https://web.stanford.edu/class/e297c/poverty_prejudice/soc_sec/hsocialsec
.htm
31
http://www.lockheedmartin.com/us/employees/healthcarereform/costs.htm
l
32 https://en.wikipedia.org/wiki/Kaiser_Permanente
33 http://news.yale.edu/2015/12/15/hospital-prices-show-mind-boggling-variation-across-us-driving-health-care-costs
34
https://www.uta.edu/faculty/story/2311/Misc/2013,2,26,MedicalCostsDemandAndGreed.pdf
35 https://www.washingtonpost.com/news/wonk/wp/2013/03/26/21-graphs-that-show-americas-health-care-prices-are-ludicrous/?utm_term=.2df65950b03d
36 http://guides.wsj.com/health/health-costs/how-to-research-health-care-prices/
37 http://www.myurgentcare365.com/wp-content/uploads/2016/07/UrgentCare365-MemberPrices.pdf
38 https://www.forbes.com/sites/rickungar/2010/09/07/the-true-cost-of-medical-malpractice-it-may-surprise-you/#733877962ff5
39 http://www.mailtribune.com/news/20170702/just-what-paramedics-ordered
40 https://www.bostonglobe.com/news/politics/2014/12/09/mit-professor-jonathan-gruber-apologizes-congress-for-remarks-about-stupidity-american-voter/AlrfLb2yWKWNTL9OvSaPFJ/story.html
41 http://www.investors.com/politics/commentary/premiums-have-steadily-climbed-despite-obama-promise-to-cut-them/
42 https://aspe.hhs.gov/system/files/pdf/256751/IndividualMarketPremiumChanges.pdf
43 http://www.forbes.com/sites/theapothecary/2015/09/28/dispelling-obamacare-cost-saving-myths/#389d76022606
44 http://www.factcheck.org/2014/04/millions-lost-insurance/
45 http://dailysignal.com/2017/03/08/debate-on-obamacare-repeal-centers-on-medicaid-heres-how-states-that-expanded-it-are-doing/
46 http://www.americanthinker.com/articles/2012/08/why_not_obamacare.html
47 https://www.congress.gov/bill/115th-congress/house-bill/1072/text
48 https://housegop.leadpages.co/healthcare/
49 The Medicare prescription drug program imposes a small penalty for failing to enter it when you become eligible. https://www.medicare.gov/part-d/costs/penalty/part-d-late-enrollment-penalty.html
50 http://time.com/4649914/why-the-doctor-takes-only-cash/
51 See https://www.ncbi.nlm.nih.gov/pmc/articles/PMC4638261/ for an extended analysis of high-cost medical care.

Appendix A: Immigration Risks

1 http://www.diabetes.org/diabetes-basics/diagnosis/
2 http://www.iihs.org/iihs/topics/t/general-statistics/fatalityfacts/state-by-state-overview
3 https://ourworldindata.org/terrorism/
4 http://www.johnstonsarchive.net/terrorism/wrjp255a.html
5 http://www.heritage.org/immigration/commentary/how-the-refugee-vetting-process-works
6 https://en.wikipedia.org/wiki/Rizwan_Farook_and_Tashfeen_Malik
7 http://www.nationalreview.com/article/448061/trump-travel-ban-ruling-fourth-circuit-sharia-supremacism-judicial-imperialism
8 http://www.people-press.org/2011/08/30/muslim-americans-no-signs-of-growth-in-alienation-or-support-for-extremism/
9 http://english.dohainstitute.org/file/Get/40ebdf12-8960-4d18-8088-7c8a077e522e   See Figure 11 and following analysis.
10 https://www.theatlantic.com/magazine/archive/2015/03/what-isis-really-wants/384980/
11 http://www.latimes.com/local/california/la-me-san-bernardino-shooting-terror-investigation-htmlstory.html
12 https://en.wikipedia.org/wiki/Shooting_of_Kathryn_Steinle
13 http://www.nationalreview.com/article/423902/welcoming-thousands-syrian-refugees-we-should-consider-what-somali-immigrants-have
14 https://en.wikipedia.org/wiki/National_Council_of_La_Raza
15 http://www.discoverthenetworks.org/printgroupProfile.asp?grpid=153
16 http://www.mayorno.com/WhoIsMecha.html
17 https://www.bloomberg.com/news/features/2018-01-17/el-komander-made-a-fortune-off-mexican-drug-ballads-now-he-s-selling-love-songs
18 https://www.commentarymagazine.com/articles/a-local-story-of-global-jihad/
19 http://www.hayk.net/destinations/glendale-ca/
20 https://en.wikipedia.org/wiki/Ileana_Ros-Lehtinen
21 http://www.migrationpolicy.org/article/family-reunification
22 https://openborders.info/moral-case/
23 Scroll to page 138 at
https://books.google.com/books?id=gMdE3uydV8AC&printsec=frontcover&dq=isbn:1596982764&hl=en&sa=X&ved=0ahUKEwjl8uPxhZHRAhUG0WMKHcrdA1IQ6AEIHDAA#v=onepage&q&f=true
24 http://evolution.berkeley.edu/evolibrary/article/history_07
25 https://www.ers.usda.gov/data-products/foreign-agricultural-trade-of-the-united-states-fatus/us-agricultural-trade-data-update/
26 http://www.gao.gov/products/GAO-14-430
27 http://www.popularmechanics.com/science/energy/g161/top-10-myths-about-natural-gas-drilling-6386593/
28 http://fortune.com/2016/10/10/donald-trump-clean-coal/

---

[29] https://www.epa.gov/burnwise/ordinances-and-regulations-wood-burning-appliances#community

Index

14th Amendment, 182
adult children, 207
adverse selection, 208
affirmative action, 173
Affordable Care Act, 130, 207
air traffic control, 55
altruism
reciprocal, 162
American Enterprise Institute, 172
anti-trust law, 119
association, 182
authoritarianism, 169
banking regulation, 123
Barney Frank, 157
Bible, 177
birthright citizenship, 87
Brotherly Love, 175
Bush, George H. W., 134
central planning, 124, 125, 126
chain immigration, 90
charities, 113
charity, 101
Christian heritage, 88
chronic conditions, 215
civil society, 31, 73
Civility, 182
command economy, 127

Commander in Chief, 68
Common Good, 73, 77
Common Law, 184, 190
Communism, 101
Community Reinvestment Act, 118
competition, 18
concept, 146
Confucius, 177
Constitution, 34
credit cards, 122
cultures, 175
democracy, 168
disability, 109, 114
education, 150
Egypt, 127
Eisenhower, President, 53
Electoral College, 169
emergence, 22, 23
emergency care, 142
Emerson, 16
Eminent domain, 118
empathy, 100
Enterprise zones, 118
entitlement, 147, 200
enumerated powers, 129
environment, 7
estate tax, 138
ethics, 21, 26
evolution, 22, 179

export subsidy, 124
Fabian Socialism, 101
factions, 151
family, 17
Fascism, 101
Federal Reserve System, 120, 121, 135
federal system, 168
Federalism, 75
Federalists, 52
First Amendment, 54
franchises, 119
freedom, 2
freedom of religion, 178
friendly societies, 101
gaming the system, 208
general welfare, 119, 201
George III, 134
Germany, 33
Gerrymandering, 173
God given rights, 19
Golden Rule, 177
good, 76
good, re ethics, 26
government, 12, 18
government guaranteed financing, 124
Gross Domestic Product (GDP), 85, 199
Gruber, Dr. Johnathon, 171
guidelines, 131
Hayek, Friedrich, 126, 211
Helmet Law, 129
Henry, Patrick, 16
Heritage Foundation, 172
honor, 5
housing subsidies, 109

illegal aliens, 87
income support, 127
income tax, 55
inflation, 134
insurance, 149, 203
Interest, 151
interstate freeways, 55
Investment, 149
ISIS, 224
Islam, 184
Jefferson, Thomas, 19
Jim Crow, 164
Laws of Nature, 19
Libertarian Party, 2, 154
libertarians, 160
license, 11
Lincoln, President, 36
living Constitution, 50
Lock, John, 16
Magna Carta, 33
majority, 169
malpractice, 206
Marine Corps, 182
market crash, 121
marriage, 185
Marx, Karl, 167
McArthur, General Douglas, 69
Medicaid, 199
Medicare, 109, 199
Moderation, 167
Mussolini, Benito, 157, 160
national unity, 127
New Deal, 57, 101
Ninth Amendment, 53
non-discretionary appropriations, 98

Obamacare, 109, 137, 171, 199
overpopulation, 229
Parks, Rosa, 181
pharmaceuticals, 205
police power, 46
political discourse, 145
pollution, 7
Ponzi, 89
population, 92
post_roads, 51
Power of the Purse, 99
pre-existing conditions, 208
price differentials, 205
prison, 68
privacy, 6, 54, 71, 217
private property, 5
private sector, 166
Progressive, 126, 132
property, 6
prudence, 69
Public Good, 77
public goods, 76
Public policy, 63
racial discrimination, 182
Rawls, John, 164
religion, 8
republic, 168
Republican Party, 172
restaurants, 185
right, 200
Roosevelt, Franklin, 57, 101
Salvation Army, 113
sanctuary, 87

Second Amendment, 54, 68, 196
self-defense, 3
Self-Esteem, 103
self-organizing, 41
sharing, 161
slavery, 12
Social Science, 59
Social Security, 58, 59, 106, 109, 110, 111, 204
Soviet Union, 126, 160
State, 38, 44
Supreme Court, 56
Talmud, 177
Technocracy, 169
Tenth Amendment, 46, 53
terrorism, 94
thought control., 184
TIAA/CREF, 111
tort, 206
Truman, President, 69, 182
underwriting, 204
undocumented migrants, 87
Universal Basic Income, 105
Universal Declaration of Human Rights, 148
Value Added Tax, 139
War on Poverty, 102
Washington, President George, 70
Wilson, Woodrow, 170, 174
Women's Suffrage, 182
WWII, 127

www.ingramcontent.com/pod-product-compliance
Lightning Source LLC
Chambersburg PA
CBHW072101020426
42334CB00017B/1592